ISBN: 9781313935050

Published by:
HardPress Publishing
8345 NW 66TH ST #2561
MIAMI FL 33166-2626

Email: info@hardpress.net
Web: http://www.hardpress.net

1. Jerusalem - Destruction, a.d. 70
2. Apologetics, Christian.

1 — JD

ZET

Holford

THE

Destruction of Jerusalem,

AN

ABSOLUTE AND IRRESISTIBLE

PROOF

OF

THE DIVINE ORIGIN

OF

CHRISTIANITY:

INCLUDING

A Narrative of the Calamities which befell the Jews, so far as they tend to verify our Lord's Predictions relative to that event.

WITH

A BRIEF DESCRIPTION OF THE CITY AND TEMPLE

~~~~~~~~~~~~~~~~

" I consider the prophecy relative to the destruction of the Jewish nation, if there were nothing else to support christianity, as absolutely irresistible "

Mr. Erskine's Speech at the Trial of Williams for publishing Paine's Age of Reason.

~~~~~~~~~~~~~~~~

FIFTH AMERICAN EDITION.

~~~~~~~~~~~~~~~~

FRANKFORD (PENN.),
PUBLISHED BY JOSEPH SHARPLESS,
T. & G. Palmer, printers.
1812.

PREFACE.

HISTORY records few events more generally interesting than the destruction of Jerusalem, and the subversion of the Jewish state, by the arms of the Romans. Their intimate connexion with the dissolution of the levitical economy, and the establishment of christianity in the world the striking verification which they afford of so many of the prophecies, both of the old and new testament, and the powerful arguments for the divine authority of the scriptures which are thence derived; the solemn warning and admonitions which they hold out to all nations, but especially to such as are favoured with the light and blessings of Revelation; together with the impressive and terrific grandeur of the events themselves—are circumstances which must always insure to the subject of the following pages more than ordinary degrees of interest and importance. Many eminent and learned men have employed their pens in the illustration of it; but the fruits of their labours are, for the most part, contained in large and expensive works, out of the reach of numbers, to whom the discussion might prove equally interesting and improving.

For the use and gratification of such, the present treatise, in a more accessible and familiar form, is diffidently offered to the public. In order that it might be better adapted to the general reader, critical inquiries and tedious details are equally avoided; but it has been the care of the writer not to omit any important fact or argument that, in his opinion, tended to elucidate the subject. Countenanced by the example of many respectable names, he has ventured to introduce the extraordinary prodigies, *which, according to* Josephus, *preceded the destruction of the* Holy City. *He has also added a few sentences in their defence, but he does not intend thereby to express his unqualified admission of their genuineness.*

Upon the execution of the tract, generally, the public will determine. Usefulness is the writer's main object; and if a perusal of it shall contribute, under the Divine Blessing, *to confirm the wavering faith of only one* christian, *or to shake the vain confidence of a single* unbeliever, *his labour will be abundantly rewarded.*

G. H.

LONDON,
January 1, 1805.

THE
DESTRUCTION OF JERUSALEM.

———

T<small>HE</small> goodness of God stamps all his pro-
ceedings. It has pleased Him not only to
communicate to mankind a revelation,
which, to the pious mind, bears in its *in-
ternal* texture its own evidence and recom-
mendation, but also to accompany it with
such *external* proofs of a sacred origin,
as seem calculated to strike, with irresistible conviction, even those who are least
disposed to admit the truth of the Holy
Scriptures. In order to evidence their
divine authenticity, God has done as much
as man could possibly have required*.

---

* This assertion is sufficient for the writer's purpose.
The fact, however, is, that the Almighty hath, in this
respect, as well as in every other, done for man " *exceed-
ing abundantly above all that*" he can " *ask or think.*" The
scheme of that evidence which demonstrates the divine
authority of the Bible could only have been constructed
by Him " *who knoweth all things, and who seeth the end from
the beginning.*"

A 2

For supposing that it had been referred to mankind to have prescribed for their own satisfaction, and that of their posterity, the credentials which His messengers should bring with them, in order to authenticate the divinity of their mission, could the wisest and the most sceptical amongst men have proposed, for this end, any thing more conclusive than,

First, Demonstrations of power, surpassing every possible effect of human skill and report——and,

Second, Intelligence relative to the future events and circumstances of nations and individuals, which no human sagacity would ever pretend to foresee or predict?

If such had been the evidences demanded, what addition to them could possibly have been suggested? Is it in the human mind to imagine any tests of divine authority better adapted, sooner or later, to expose the artifices, and frustrate the designs, of an impostor? In vain will the profoundest policy attempt to discover means more suitable to this purpose, and, with respect to the reception of the revelation itself, more perfectly fitted to banish all reasonable doubt on the one hand, and to invalidate the charge of credulity on the other. Now these, precisely, are the credentials with which it has pleased God to sanction the testimony of his inspired messengers, as recorded in the Scriptures of the Old and New Testaments. *They wrought miracles: they foretold future events.* Thus all that man himself could demand has been given, and objectors are left entirely without excuse.

Jesus Christ, the principal of those messengers, like his illustrious types and predecessors Moses and Elijah, proclaimed and attested his divine mission at once by miraculous acts, and by prophetic declarations.. His miracles were numerous, di-

versified, and performed in various parts
of his native country : they were not fri-
volous tricks, calculated merely to excite
wonder, and gratify curiosity, but acts
of substantial utility and benevolence.
They were publicly, but not boastingly
nor ostentatiously displayed : in the presence not of friends only, but also of enemies—of enemies exasperated to malignity against him, because he had censured
their vices and exposed their hypocrisy,
and who were actuated by every motive
which a spirit of revenge could suggest to
incurable prejudice, to induce them to de-
tect the imposition of his miracles, if *false*,
and to deny and discredit them, if *true*. To
deny them they did not attempt, but they
strove to sink them in disrepute, and thereby furnished a striking specimen of those
embarrassing dilemmas, into which infidelity is continually betraying her votaries.
They ascribed them to the agency of Satan ; thus representing him, " *who was a
liar from the beginning*," as contributing

to the diffusion of truth—" *the spirit that worketh in the children of disobedience*" as promoting the cause of holiness, and as co-operating in the overthrow of *his own kingdom*, with Him " *who was manifested to destroy the works of the devil!*"

The prophecies of our Lord, as well as his miracles, were many, and of great variety. They were not delivered with pomp and parade, but rose out of occasions, and seem to have resulted, for the most part, from his affectionate solicitude for those who then were, or who might afterwards become, his disciples. While the fulfilment of some of these predictions was confined to the term of his mission and the limits of his country, the accomplishment of others extended to all nations, and to every future age of the world.

Of the prophecies which have already been fulfilled, few, perhaps, are so interesting in themselves, or so striking in

their accomplishment as those which relate to the *destruction of Jerusalem and its
temple*, and the signal calamities which
every where befel the Jewish nation.   The
chief of our Lord's predictions, relative to
these events, are contained in Matt. xxiv.
Mark xiii. Luke xix. 41-44; xxi. and
xxiii. 27-30:   and we may with confidence appeal to the *facts* which verify
them as conclusive and incontrovertible
proofs of the divinity of his mission.   Before, however, we enter upon this illustration, it may be gratifying to the reader,
and add considerably to the interest of
many of the subsequent pages, to give in
this place a brief description of that re-
nowned city and its temple.

Jerusalem was built on two mountains.
Three celebrated walls surrounded the
city on every side, except that which was
deemed inaccessible, and there it was defended by one wall only.   The most ancient of these walls was remarkable for

its great strength, and was, moreover, erected on a hanging rock, and fortified by sixty towers. On the middle wall there were fourteen towers only; but on the third, which was also distinguished by the extraordinary merit of its architecture, there were no less than ninety. The celebrated tower of Psephinos, before which Titus at first encamped, was erected on this latter wall, and even excelled it in the superior style of its architecture: it was seventy cubits high, and had eight angles, each of which commanded most extensive and beautiful prospects. In clear weather, the spectator had from them a view of the Mediterranean sea, of Arabia, and of the whole extent of the Jewish dominions. Besides this, there were three other towers of great magnitude, named Hippocos, Phasael, and Mariamne. The two former, famed for their strength and grandeur, were near ninety cubits high; the latter, for its valuable curiosities, beauty, and elegance, was about fifty-five cubits. They were all built of white marble; and so exquisite was the workmanship, that each of them appeared as if it had been hewn out of an immense single block of it. Notwithstanding their great elevation, they yet must have appeared, from the surrounding country, far loftier than they really were. The old wall, it has just been remarked, was built upon a high rock : but these towers were erected on the *top* of a hill, the summit of which was itself thirty cubits above the *top* of the old wall! Such edifices, so situated, it is easy to conceive, must have given to the city a very great degree of grandeur and magnificence. Not far distant from these towers stood the royal palace, of singular beauty and elegance. Its pillars, its porticoes, its galleries, its apartments, were all incredibly costly, splendid, and superb; while t c groves, gardens, walks, fountains, and aqueducts, with which it was encompassed, formed the richest and most delightful scenery that can possibly be imagined. The situation of these structures was on the north side of Jerusalem, Its celebrated temple, and the strong fort of Antonia, were on the east side, and directly opposite to the Mount of Olives. This fort was built on a rock fifty cubits in height, and so steep as to be inaccessible on every side ; and to render it still more so, it was faced with thin slabs of marble, which, being slippery, proved at once a defence and an ornament. In the midst of the fort stood the castle of Antonia, the interior parts of which, for grandeur, state, and convenience, resembled more a palace than a fortress. Viewed from a distance, it had the appearance of a tower, encompassed by four other towers, situated at the four angles of a square. Of these latter, three were fifty cubits high, and the fourth seventy cubits.

The tower last mentioned commanded an excellent view of the whole temple, the

B

riches, grandeur, and elegance of which, it is not in the power of language to describe. Whether we consider its architecture, its dimensions, its magnificence, its splendour, or the sacred purposes to which it was dedicated, it must equally be regarded as the most astonishing fabric that was ever constructed. It was erected partly on a solid rock, which was originally steep on every side. The foundations of what was called the lower temple were three hundred cubits in depth, and the stones of which they were composed, more than sixty feet in length, while the superstructure contained, of the whitest marble, stones nearly sixty-eight feet long, more than seven feet high, and nine broad. The circuit of the whole building was four furlongs; its height one hundred cubits; one hundred and sixty pillars, each twenty-seven feet high, ornamented and sustained the immense and ponderous edifice. In the front, spacious and lofty galleries, wainscotted with cedar, were supported by columns of white marble, in uniform rows.   In short, says Josephus, nothing could surpass even the exterior of this temple, for its elegant and curious workmanship. It was adorned with solid plates of gold that rivalled the beauty of the rising sun, and were scarcely less dazzling to the eye than the beams of that luminary.   Of those parts of the building which were not gilt, when viewed from a distance, some, says he, appeared like *pillars of snow*, and some like *mountains of white marble*.   The splendour of the interior parts of the temple, corresponded with its external magnificence.   It was decorated and enriched by every thing that was costly, elegant, and superb.   Religious donations and offerings had poured into this wonderful repository of precious stores from every part of the world, during many successive ages.   In the lower temple was placed those sacred curiosities, the seven-branched candlestick of pure gold, the table for the shew-bread, and the altar of incense; the two latter of which were covered over with plates of the same metal. In the sanctuary were several doors, fifty-five cubits high, and sixteen in breadth, which were all likewise of gold. Before these doors hung a veil of the most beautiful Babylonian tapestry, composed of scarlet, blue, and purple, exquisitely interwoven, and wrought up to the highest degree of art. From the top of the ceiling depended branches and leaves of vines, and large clusters of grapes hanging down five or six feet, all of gold, and of most admirable workmanship. In addition to these proofs of the splendour and riches of the temple, may be noticed its eastern gate of pure Corinthian brass, more esteemed even than the precious metals—the golden folding-doors of the chambers—the beautiful carved work, gilding, and painting of the galleries—the golden vessels, &c. of the sanctuary, the sacerdotal vestments of scarlet, violet, and purple—the vast wealth of the treasury—

abundance of precious stones, and immense quantities of all kinds of costly spices and perfumes. In short, the most valuable and sumptuous of whatever nature, or art, or opulence could supply, was enclosed within the consecrated walls of this magnificent and venerable edifice.

So much concerning this celebrated city, and its still more celebrated temple. We shall now consider our Lord's prophecies relating to their destruction.

On the Monday immediately preceding his crucifixion, our blessed Saviour made his public and triumphant entry into Jerusalem, amidst the acclamations of a very great multitude of his disciples, who hailed him *King of Sion*, and with palm branches, the emblems of victory, in their hands, rejoiced and gave praises to God for all the mighty works that they had seen, singing " *Hosannah! blessed be the King that cometh in the name of the*

B 2

Lord! Peace in heaven, and glory in the highest!" But while the people thus exulted and triumphantly congratulated their Messiah, he, struggling with the deepest emotions of pity and compassion for Jerusalem, beheld the city and wept over it, saying, " *If thou hadst known, even thou, at least in this thy day, the things which belong unto thy peace! but now they are hid from thine eyes; for the days shall come upon thee, that thine enemies shall cast a trench about thee, and compass thee round, and keep thee in on every side; and shall lay thee even with the ground, and thy children within thee: and they shall not leave in thee one stone upon another; because thou knewest not the time of thy visitation*."
On the Wednesday following, being only two days before his death, he went for the last time into the temple to teach the people; while he was thus employed, the High Priests and the Elders, the Herodians, Saducees, and Pharisees, succes-

* Luke, xix. 42—44.

sively came to him, and questioned him
with subtilty, being desirous to " *entangle*
him in his talk ;" to whom, with his ac-
customed dignity and wisdom, he returned answers which carried conviction to
their hearts, and at once silenced and
astonished them. Then, turning to his
disciples, and the whole multitude, he
addressed to them a discourse of very uncommon energy, in which, with most exquisite keenness of reproof, he exposed
and condemned the cruelty and pride, the
hypocrisy and sensuality of the Pharisees
and Scribes. Having next foretold the
barbarous treatment which his apostles
would receive at their hands, he proceeded to denounce against Jerusalem the dire
and heavy vengeance, that had for ages
been accumulating in the vials of divine
displeasure, expressly declaring, that it
should be poured out upon the *then existing generation*, adding that inimitably
tender and pathetic apostrophe to this devoted city, " *O, Jerusalem, Jerusalem!*

thou that killest the prophets, and stonest them which are sent unto thee, how often would I have gathered thy children together, even as a hen gathereth her chickens under her wings, and ye would not! Behold! your house is left unto you desolate; for I say unto you, ye shall not see me henceforth, till ye shall say, Blessed is he that cometh in the name of the Lord*!" Having said this, he went out of the temple, and, as he departed, his disciples drew his attention to the wonderful magnitude and splendour of the edifice. They spake, *" how it was adorned with goodly stones and gifts;"* and said unto him, *" Master, see what manner of stones and buildings are here! And Jesus said unto them, See ye not all these things? Verily, I say unto you, there shall not be left here one stone upon another, that shall not be thrown down."* When we consider the antiquity and sanctity of the temple, its stupendous fabric, its solidity, and the uncommon

---

* Mat. xxiii. 37—39.

magnitude of the stones of which it was composed, we may, in some measure, conceive of the amazement which this declaration of our Lord must have excited in the minds of his disciples. Nevertheless, this remarkable prediction, as we shall see in the sequel, was *literally* fulfilled, and as our Lord had foretold, even during the existence of the generation to which he addressed it.

Our Lord now retired to the Mount of Olives, to which place the disciples followed him, in order to make more particular inquiries relative to the time when the calamitous events, foretold by him, would come to pass. We have already intimated, that the Mount of Olives commanded a full view of Jerusalem and the temple. No situation, therefore, could have been better adapted to give energy to a prediction which related chiefly to their total ruin and demolition; and if we suppose (and the supposition is highly probable) that our Lord, while in the act of speaking, pointed to the majestic and stupendous edifices, whose destruction he foretold, every word which he then uttered must have been clothed with inexpressible sublimity, and derived, from the circumstances of the surrounding scenery, a force and effect, which it is not possible adequately to conceive.

" *Tell us, when shall these things be? and what shall be the* sign *when all these things shall be fulfilled?*"   Such were the questions of the disciples, in answer to which our Lord condescended to give them a particular account of the several important events that would precede, as well as of the prognostics which would announce the approaching desolations; including suitable directions for the regulation of their conduct under the various trials to which they were to be exposed. He commences with a caution: " *Take heed,*" says he, " *that no man deceive you;*

!

*for many shall come in my name, saying,
I am Christ, and shall deceive many.*" The
necessity for this friendly warning soon
appeared; for within one year after our
Lord's ascension, rose Dositheus, the Sa-
maritan, who had the boldness to assert
that he was the Messiah of whom Moses
prophesied; while his disciple, Simon Ma-
gus, deluded multitudes into a belief that
he himself was the *great power of God.*
About three years afterwards, another Sa-
maritan impostor appeared, and declared
that he would show the people the sacred
utensils, said to have been deposited by
Moses in Mount Gerizim. Induced by
an idea that the Messiah, their great deliverer, was now come, an armed multitude assembled under him; but Pilate
speedily defeated them, and slew their
chief. While Cuspius Fadus was pro-
curator in Judea, another deceiver arose,
whose name was Theudas*. This man
actually succeeded so far as to persuade

* This is not the Theudas mentioned by Gamaliel,
Acts, v. 36.

a very great multitude to take their effects
and follow him to Jordan, assuring them,
that the river would divide at his command.   Fadus, however, pursued them,
with a troop of horse, and slew many of
them, and, among the rest, the impostor
himself, whose head was cut off, and carried to Jerusalem.   Under the government of Felix, deceivers rose up daily in
Judea, and persuaded the people to follow them into the wilderness, assuring
them that they should there behold con-
spicuous signs and wonders performed by
the Almighty.   Of these, Felix, from
time to time, apprehended many, and put
them to death.   About this period (A. D.
55), arose Felix, the celebrated Egyptian
impostor, who collected thirty thousand
followers, and persuaded them to accompany him to the Mount of Olives, telling
them that from thence they should see the
walls of Jerusalem fall down at his command, as a prelude to the capture of the
Roman garrison, and to their obtaining

the sovereignty of the city.   The Roman governor, however, apprehending this to be the beginning of revolt, immediately attacked them, slew four hundred of them, and dispersed the rest; but the Egyptian effected his escape.   In the time of Porcius Festus (A. D. 60), another distinguished impostor seduced the people, by promising them deliverance from the Roman yoke, if they would follow him into the wilderness; but Festus sent out an armed force, which speedily destroyed both the deceiver and his followers.   In short, impostors, pretending to a divine commission, continually and fatally deceived the people, and at once justified the caution, and fulfilled the prediction of our Lord.

If it be objected, that none of these impostors, except Dositheus, assumed the name of Messiah, we reply, that the grovelling expectation of the Jews was directed to a Messiah who should merely deli-

c

ver them from the Roman yoke, and " *re-store the kingdom to Jerusalem;*" and such were the pretensions of these deceivers.   This expectation, indeed, is the only true solution of these strange and repeated insurrections; which will naturally remind the reader of the following prophetic expressions of our Lord : " *I am come in my Father's name, and ye receive me not ; if another shall come in his own name, him ye will receive.*" " *If they shall say unto you, behold, he is in the desert, go not forth.   They will show** (or pretend to show) *great signs and won-ders,*" &c.

Our Saviour thus proceeded : " *And ye shall hear of wars, and rumours of wars: see that ye be not troubled : for all these things must come to pass, but the end is not yet, for nation shall rise up against na-*

---

* The original word signifies " give ;" and that, in Scripture language, there is a clear distinction betwixt *giving a sign* and the *sign itself*, is sufficiently proved by Deut. xiii. 1, 2.

tion, and kingdom against kingdom, and great earthquakes shall be in divers places, and famines, and pestilences : all these are the beginning of sorrows*."

" *Wars and rumours of wars,*" &c. These commotions, like distant thunder, that forebodes the approaching storm,

" At first heard solemn o'er the verge of heaven,"

were so frequent from the death of our Lord until the destruction of Jerusalem, that the whole interval might, with propriety, be appealed to in illustration of this prophecy. One hundred and fifty of the copious pages of Josephus, which contain the history of this period, are every where stained with blood. To particularize in a few instances : About three years after the death of Christ, a war broke out between Herod and Aretas, king of Arabia Petræa, in which the army of the former was cut off. This was " *kingdom rising against kingdom.*" Wars are usually pre-

---

* Mat. xxiv. 6—8. Luke xxi. 11.

ceded by rumours. It may, therefore, appear absurd to attempt a distinct elucidation of this part of the prophecy ; nevertheless, it ought not to be omitted, that about this time the emperor Caligula, having ordered his statue to be placed in the temple of Jerusalem, and the Jews having persisted to refuse him, the whole nation were so much alarmed, by the mere apprehension of war, that they neglected even to till their lands ! The storm, however, blew over.

About this period, a great number of Jews, on account of a pestilence which raged at Babylon, removed from that city to Selucia, where the Greeks and Syrians rose against them, and destroyed of this devoted people more than five myriads ! " The extent of this slaughter," says Josephus, " had no parallel in any former period of their history." Again, about five years after this dreadful massacre, there happened a severe contest between

the Jews at Perea and the Philadel-
phians, respecting the limits of a city
called Mia, in which many of the former were slain. This was "*nation rising
up against nation.*" Four years afterwards, under Cumanus, an indignity
was offered to the Jews within the pre-
cincts of the temple, by a Roman soldier,
which they violently resented ; but upon
the approach of the Romans in great force,
their terror was so excessive, and so dis-
orderly and precipitate their flight, that
not less than ten thousand Jews were trodden to death in the streets. This, again,
was "*nation rising up against nation.*"
Four years more had not elapsed, before
the Jews made war against the Samaritans,
and ravaged their country. The people
of Samaria had murdered a Galilean,
who was going up to Jerusalem to keep
the passover, and the Jews thus revenged
it. At Cæsarea, the Jews having had a
sharp contention with the Syrians for the
government of the city, an appeal was

made to Nero, who decreed it to the Sy
rians.   This event laid the foundation of a
most cruel and sanguinary contest between
the two nations.   The Jews, mortified by
disappointment, and inflamed by jealousy,
rose against the Syrians, who successful
ly repelled them.   In the city of Cæsarea alone, upwards of twenty thousand
Jews were slain.   The flame, however, was
not now quenched; it spread its destruc
tive rage wherever the Jews and Syrians
dwelt together in the same place: through
out every city, town, and village, mutual
animosity and slaughter prevailed.   At
Damascus, Tyre, Ascalon, Gadara, and
Scythopolis, the carnage was dreadful.   At
the first of these cities ten thousand Jews
were slain in one hour, and at Scythopolis
thirteen thousand treacherously in one
night.   At Alexandria, the Jews, aggriev-
ed by the oppressions of the Romans, rose
against them ; but the Romans, gaining
the ascendency, slew of that nation fifty
thousand persons, sparing neither infants

nor the aged. And after this, at the siege of Jotapata, not less than forty thousand Jews perished. While these destructive contests prevailed in the East the western parts of the Roman empire were rent by the fierce contentions of Galba, Otho, and Vitellius; of which three emperors it is remarkable, that they all, together with Nero, their immediate predecessor, died a violent death, within the short space of eighteen months. Finally, the whole nation of the Jews took up arms against the Romans, king Agrippa, &c. and provoked that dreadful war which, in a few years, deluged Judea with blood, and laid its capital in ruins.

If it be here objected, that, because wars are events of frequent occurrence, it would be improper to refer to supernatural foresight a successful prediction respecting them, it is replied, that much of this objection will be removed, by considering the incompetency of even statesmen them-

selves to foretell the condition, only for a
few years, of the very nation whose affairs
they administer.   It is a well-known fact,
that the present minister of Great Britain,
on the very eve of the late long and destructive war with the French Republic,
held out to his country a picture of fifteen
successive years of peace and prosperity.
Indeed, the nice points on which peace
and war often depend, baffle all calculations from present aspects; and a rumour
of war, so loud and so alarming as even
to suspend the operations of husbandry,
may terminate, as we have just seen, in
nothing but rumour.   Further, let it be
considered, that the wars to which this
part of our Lord's prophecy referred, were
to be of two kinds, and that the event corresponded accordingly;   that they occurred within the period to which he had assigned them ; that they fell with the most
destructive severity on the Jews ; to whom
the prophecy at large chiefly related, and
that the person who predicted them was

not in the condition of a statesman, but in that of a carpenter's son! On this subject more in another place.

" *And great earthquakes shall be in divers places.*" Of these significant emblems of political commotions, there occurred several within the scene of this prophecy, and, as our Saviour predicted, in divers places. In the reign of Claudius, there was one at Rome, and another at Apamea, in Syria, where many of the Jews resided. The earthquake at the latter place was so destructive, that the emperor, in order to relieve the distresses of the inhabitants, remitted its tribute for five years. Both these earthquakes are recorded by Tacitus. There was one also, in the same reign, in Crete. This is mentioned by Philostratus, in his life of Apollonius, who says, that there were others " at Smyrna, Miletus, Chios, and Samos; in all which places Jews had settled." In the reign of Nero there was an earthquake

at Laodicea. Tacitus records this also.
It is likewise mentioned by Eusebius and
Orosius, who add, that Hierapolis and Colosse, as well as Laodicea, were over-
thrown by an earthquake. There was
also one in Campania in this reign (of this
both Tacitus and Seneca speak); and
another at Rome in the reign of Galba, recorded by Suetonius; to all which may
be added those which happened on that
dreadful night when the Idumeans were
excluded from Jerusalem, a short time before the siege commenced. " A heavy
storm (says Josephus) burst on them during the night; violent winds arose, accompanied with the most excessive rains, with
constant lightnings, most tremendous thun-
derings, and with dreadful roarings of
earthquakes. It seemed (continues he)
as if the system of the world had been
confounded for the destruction of mankind; and one might well conjecture that
these were signs of no common events!"

Our Lord predicted " *famines*" also. Of these the principal was that which Agabus foretold would happen in the days of Claudius, as related in the Acts of the Apostles. It began in the fourth year of his reign, and was of long continuance. It extended through Greece, and even into Italy, but was felt most severely in Judea, and especially at Jerusalem, where many perished for want of bread. This famine is recorded by Josephus also, who relates that an assaron of corn was sold for 5 drachmæ (i. e. about 3 pints and a half for 3s. 3d.). It is likewise noticed by Eusebius and Orosius. To alleviate this terrible calamity, Helena, queen of Adiabena, who was at that time in Jerusalem, ordered large supplies of grain to be sent from Alexandria; and Izates, her son, consigned vast sums to the governors of Jerusalem, to be applied to the relief of the more indigent sufferers. The Gentile christian converts residing in foreign countries, also sent, at the instance of St.

Paul, liberal contributions to relieve the distresses of their Jewish brethren*. Dion Cassius relates that there was likewise a famine in the first year of Claudius, which prevailed at Rome, and in other parts of Italy; and, in the eleventh year of the same emperor, there was another, mentioned by Eusebius. To these may be added those that afflicted the inhabitants of several of the cities of Galilee and Judea, which were besieged and taken, previously to the investment of Jerusalem, where the climax of national misery, arising from this and every other cause, was so awfully completed.

Our Saviour adds "*pestilences*" likewise. Pestilence treads upon the heels of famine; it may therefore reasonably be presumed, that this terrible scourge accompanied the famines which had just been enumerated. History, however, particularly distinguishes two instances of

---

* 1 Corin. xvi. 3.

this calamity, which occurred before the commencement of the Jewish war. The first took place at Babylon, about A. D. 40, and raged so alarmingly, that great multitudes of Jews fled from that city to Seleucia for safety, as hath been hinted already. The other happened at Rome, A. D. 65, and carried off prodigious multitudes. Both Tacitus and Suetonius also record, that similar calamities prevailed, during this period, in various other parts of the Roman empire. After Jerusalem was surrounded by the army of Titus, pestilential diseases soon made their appearance there, to aggravate the miseries, and deepen the horrors of the siege. They were partly occasioned by the immense multitudes which were crowded together in the city, partly by the putrid effluvia which arose from the unburied dead, and partly from the prevalence of the famine.

Our Lord proceeded: " *And fearful sights and great signs shall there be from*

D

heaven*."—Josephus has collected the chief of these portents together, and introduces his account by a reflection on the strangeness of that infatuation, which could induce his countrymen to give credit to impostors, and unfounded reports, whilst they disregarded the divine admonitions, confirmed, as he asserts they were, by the following extraordinary signs :

1. " A meteor, resembling a sword†, hung over Jerusalem during one whole year." This could not be a comet, for it was stationary, and was visible for twelve successive months. A sword, too, though a fit emblem of destruction, but ill represents a comet.

2. " On the eighth of the month Zanthicus (before the feast of unleavened bread), at the ninth hour of the night, there shone round about the altar, and the circumjacent buildings of the temple, a light equal

---

* Luke xxi. 11.   † Vide 1 Chron. xxi. 15.

to the brightness of the day, which continued for the space of half an hour." This
could not be the effect of lightning, nor of
a vivid *aurora borealis*, for it was confined
to a particular spot, and the light shone un-
intermittedly thirty minutes.

3. " As the High Priests were leading
a heifer to the altar to be sacrificed, she
brought forth a lamb, in the midst of the
temple." Such is the strange account
given by the historian. Some may regard
it as " a Grecian fable;" while others
may think that they discern in this prodigy a miraculous rebuke of Jewish infidelity and impiety, for rejecting that an-
titypical Lamb, who had offered Himself
as an atonement, " once for all;" and
who, by thus completely fulfilling their
design, had virtually abrogated the Levitical sacrifices. However this may be, the
circumstances of the prodigy are remarkable. It did not occur in an obscure part
of the city, but in the temple; not at an

ordinary time, but at the Passover, the season of our Lord's crucifixion—in the presence, not of the vulgar merely, but of the High Priests and their attendants, and when they were leading the sacrifice to the altar.

4. " About the sixth hour of the night, the eastern gate of the temple was seen to open without human assistance." When the guards informed the curator of this event, he sent men to assist them in shutting it, who with great difficulty succeeded. This gate, as hath been observed already, was of solid brass, and required twenty men to close it every evening. It could not have been opened by a " strong gust of wind," or a " slight earthquake ;" for Josephus says, " it was secured by iron bolts and bars, which were let down into a large threshold, consisting of one entire stone*."

---

* The conclusion which the Jews drew from this event was, that the security of the temple was gone.

5. " Soon after the feast of the Passover, in various parts of the country, before the setting of the sun, chariots and
armed men were seen in the air, passing
round about Jerusalem." Neither could
this portentous spectacle be occasioned
by the *aurora borealis*, for it occurred before the setting of the sun ; or merely the
fancy of a few villagers, gazing at the
heavens, for it was seen in various parts
of the country.

6. " At the subsequent feast of Pentecost, while the priests were going, by
night, into the inner temple to perform
their customary ministrations, they first
felt, as they said, a shaking, accompanied
by an indistinct murmuring, and afterwards voices as of a multitude, saying, in
a distinct and earnest manner,—' Let us
depart hence'." This gradation will remind the reader of that awful transaction,
which the feast of Pentecost was princi-
pally instituted to commemorate. First,

D 2

a shaking was heard; this would naturally induce the priests to listen; an unintel-
ligible murmuring succeeds; this would
more powerfully arrest their attention—
and while it was thus awakened and fixed,
they heard, says Josephus, the voices, as
of a multitude, distinctly pronouncing the
words "Let us depart hence." And accordingly, before the period for celebrat-
ing this feast returned, the Jewish war
had commenced, and in the space of three
years afterwards, Jerusalem was surrounded by the Roman army, the temple
converted into a citadel, and its sacred
courts streaming with the blood of human
victims.

7. As the last and most fearful omen,
Josephus relates that one Jesus, the son of
Ananus, a rustic of the lower class, during
the feast of tabernacles, suddenly exclaimed in the temple, "A voice from the east
—a voice from the west—a voice from the
four winds—a voice against Jerusalem and

the temple—a voice against bridegrooms and brides—a voice against the whole people!" These words he incessantly proclaimed aloud both day and night, through all the streets of Jerusalem, for seven years and five months together, commencing at a time (A. D. 62) when the city was in a state of peace and over-flowing with prosperity, and terminating amidst the horrors of the siege. This disturber, having excited the attention of the magistracy, was brought before Albinus, the Roman governor, who command-ed that he should be scourged. But the severest stripes drew from him neither tears nor supplications. As he never thanked those who relieved, so neither did he complain of the injustice of those who struck him. And no other answer could the governor obtain to his interrogatories, but his usual denunciation of " Wo, wo to Jerusalem !" which he still continued to proclaim through the city, but especi-ally during the festivals, when his manner became more earnest, and the tone of his voice louder. At length, on the commencement of the siege, he ascended the walls, and, in a more powerful voice than ever, exclaimed, "Wo, wo to this city, this temple, and this people!" And then, with a presentiment of his own death, added, "Wo, wo to myself!" He had scarcely uttered these words, when a stone from one of the Roman engines killed him on the spot.

Such are the prodigies related by Josephus, and which, excepting the first, he places in the year immediately preceding the Jewish war. Several of them are recorded also by Tacitus. Nevertheless, it ought to be observed, that they are received by christian writers cautiously, and with various degrees of credit. Those, however, who are most sceptical, and who resolve them into natural causes, allow the " superintendance of God to awaken his people by some of these

means." Whatever the fact, in this respect, may be, it is clear that they corresponded to our Lord's prediction of "*fearful sights, and great signs from heaven;*"
and ought to be deemed a sufficient answer to the objector, who demands, whether any such appearances are respectably
recorded.

The next prediction of our Lord related
to the persecutions of his disciples: "*They
shall lay their hands on you,*" said he,
"*and persecute you, delivering you up to
the synagogues and into prisons, being
brought before kings and rulers for my
name's sake*;*" "*and they shall deliver
you up to councils, and in the synagogues
ye shall be beaten†;*" "*and some of you
shall they cause to be put to death‡.*"
In the very infancy of the christian church,
these unmerited and unprovoked cruelties
began to be inflicted. Our Lord, and his
forerunner John the Baptist, had already

* Luke xxi. 12. † Mark xiii. 9. ‡ Luke xxi. 16.

been put to death; the apostles Peter and John were first imprisoned, and then, together with the other apostles, were scourged before the Jewish council; Stephen, after confounding the Sanhedrim with his irresistible eloquence, was stoned to death; Herod Agrippa " *stretched forth his hands to vex certain of the church,*" beheaded James the brother of John, and again imprisoned Peter, designing to put him to death also; St. Paul pleaded before the Jewish council at Jerusalem, and before Felix, the Roman governor, who trembled on the judgment seat, while the intrepid prisoner " *reasoned of righteousness, temperance, and judgment to come!*" Two years afterwards, he was brought before the tribunal of Festus (who had succeeded Felix in the government), king Agrippa the younger being present, who, while the governor scoffed, ingenuously acknowledged the force of the apostle's eloquence, and, half convinced, exclaimed, " *Almost thou persuadest me to be a* *christian.*" Lastly, he pleaded before the emperor Nero at Rome; he was also brought with Silas before the rulers at Philippi, where both of them were scourged and imprisoned. Paul was likewise imprisoned two years in Judea, and afterwards twice at Rome, each time for the space of two years. He was scourged by the Jews five times, thrice beaten with rods, and once stoned; nay, he himself, before his conversion, was an instrument of fulfilling these predictions. St. Luke relates of him, that " *he made havoc of the church, entering into every house. and haling men and women, committed them to prison; when they were put to death. he gave his voice gainst them; he punished them oft in every synagogue, and persecuted them even into strange cities;*" and to this agree his own declarations*. At length, about two years before the Jewish war, the first general persecution commenced at the instigation of the emperor Nero, " who,"

* *Vide* Acts xxvi. 10, 11. Gal. i. 23.

says Tacitus, " inflicted upon the christians, punishments exquisitely painful ;"
multitudes suffered a cruel martyrdom,
amidst derision and insults, and among
the rest the venerable apostles St. Peter
and St. Paul.

Our Lord continues—" *And ye shall be
hated of all nations for my name's sake**."
The hatred from which the above recited
persecutions sprang, was not provoked on
the part of the christians, by a contuma-
cious resistance to established authority,
or by any violations of law, but was the
unavoidable consequence of their sustain-
ing the name, and imitating the example
of their Master. " It was a war," says
Tertullian, " against the very name ; to
be a christian was of itself crime enough."
And to the same effect is that expression
of Pliny in his letter to Trajan ; " I asked
them whether they were christians ; if
they confessed it, I asked them a second

* Mat. xxiv. 9.

and a third time, threatening them with punishment, and those who persevered I commanded to be led away to death.—It is added, " *Of all nations.*" Whatever animosity or dissentions might subsist between the Gentiles and the Jews on other points, they were at all times ready to unite and to co-operate in the persecution of the humble followers of Him, who came to be a light to the former, and the glory of the latter.

" *And then shall many be offended, and shall betray one another**." Concerning this fact, the following decisive testimony of Tacitus may suffice : speaking of the persecutions of the christians under Nero, to which we have just alluded, he adds, " several were seized, who confessed, and by their discovery a great multitude of others were convicted and barbarously executed."

---

* Matt. xxiv. 10.

E

" *And the Gospel of the kingdom shall be preached in all the world, for a witness unto all nations, and then shall the end* (i. e. of the Jewish dispensation) *come*.*" —Of the fulfilment of this prediction, the Epistles of St. Paul, addressed to the christians at Rome, Corinth, Galatia, Ephesus, Phillippi, Colosse, Thessalonica, and those of Peter, to such as resided in Pontus, Cappadocia, and Bythynia, are monuments now standing; for neither of these Apostles were living when the Jewish war commenced. St. Paul too, in his Epistle to the Romans, informs them that " *their faith was spoken of throughout the world;*" and in that to the Colossians he observes, that the " Gospel had been preached to every creature under heaven." Clement, who was a fellow-labourer with the Apostle, relates of him that " he taught the whole world righteousness, travelling from the east westward to the borders of the ocean." Eusebius says

---

* Mat. xxiv. 14.

CHRISTIANITY IN THE WORLD. 5'

that " the Apostles preached the Gospel in all the world, and that some of them passed beyond the bounds of the ocean, and visited the Britannic isles* :" so says Theodoret also.

" It appears," says Bishop Newton, " from the writers of the history of the church, that before the destruction of Jerusalem, the Gospel was not only preached in the Lesser Asia, and Greece, and Italy, the great theatres of action then in the world, but was likewise propagated as far northward as Scythia, as far southward as Ethiopia, as far eastward as Parthia and India, as far westward as Spain and Britain." And Tacitus asserts, that " the christian religion, which arose in Judea, spread over many parts of the world, and

---

* It is admitted that the phrases " all the world," " every creature," &c. are hyperbolical ; but then, taken in their connexion, they evidently import the universality of the preaching and spread of the Gospel, previously to the destruction of Jerusalem, which was the point to be proved.

extended to Rome itself, where the pro-
fessors of it, as early as the time of Nero,
amounted to a vast multitude," insomuch
that their numbers excited the jealousy of
the government.

Thus completely was fulfilled a prediction contrary to every conclusion that
could have been grounded on moral pro-
bability, and to the accomplishment of
which every kind of impediment was incessantly opposed. The reputed son of a
mechanic instructs a few simple fishermen
in a new religion, destitute of worldly in-
centives, but full of self-denials, sacrifices,
and sufferings, and tells them that in about
forty years it should spread over all the
world. It spreads accordingly; and, in
defiance of the exasperated bigotry of the
Jews, and of all the authority, power, and
active opposition of the Gentiles, is established, within that period, in all the countries into which it penetrates. Can any one

doubt but that the prediction and its fulfilment were equally divine?

Such, briefly, is the account that history
gives of the several events and signs,
which our Lord had foretold would precede the destruction of the Holy City.
No sooner were his predictions accomplished, than a most unaccountable infatuation seized upon the whole Jewish nation;
so that they not only provoked, but seemed
even to rush into the midst of those unpa-
ralleled calamities, which at length totally
overwhelmed them. In an essay of this
sort it is impossible to enter into a minute
detail of the origin and progress of these
evils; but such particulars as illustrate
the fulfilment of the remaining part of the
prophecy, and justify the strong language
in which it is couched, shall be presented
to the reader.

From the conquest of their country by
Pompey, about 60 years B. C. the Jews

had, on several occasions, manifested a re-
fractory spirit; but after Judas the Gaulo-
nite and Sadduc the Pharisee had taught
them, that submission to the Roman as-
sessments would pave the way to a state
of abject slavery, this temper displayed
itself with increasing malignity and vio-
lence.   Rebellious tumults and insurrections became more and more frequent and
alarming; and to these the mercenary ex-
actions of Florus, the Roman governor,
not a little contributed.   At length Eleazer, son of the high priest, persuaded
those who officiated in the temple to reject
the sacrifices of foreigners, and no longer
to offer up prayers for them.   Thus an
insult was thrown upon Cæsar, his sacrifice rejected, and the foundation of the
Roman war laid.   The disturbances among
the Jews still continuing, Cestius Gallus,
president of Syria, marched an army into
Judea, in order to quell them, and his
career was every where marked with blood
and desolation.   As he proceeded, he plun-

dered and burnt the beautiful city of Zabulon, Joppa, and all the villages which lay in his way. At Joppa, he slew of the inhabitants eight thousand four hundred. He laid waste the district of Narbatene; and, sending an army into Galilee, slew there two thousand of the seditious Jews. He then burnt the city of Lydda; and after having repulsed the Jews, who made a desperate sally upon him, encamped at length at the distance of about one mile from Jerusalem. On the fourth day he entered its gates, and burnt three divisions of the city, and might now, by its capture, have put a period to the war; but through the treacherous persuasions of his officers, instead of pursuing his advantages, he most unaccountably raised the siege, and fled from the city with the utmost precipitation. The Jews, however, pursued him as far as Antipatris, and, with little loss to themselves, slew of his army nearly six thousand men. After this disaster had befallen Cestius, the mor-

opulent of the Jews, says Josephus, forsook Jerusalem as men do a sinking ship.
And it is with reason supposed, that on
this occasion many of the Christians, or
converted Jews, who dwelt there, recol-
lecting the warnings of their divine Master, retired to Pella, a place beyond Jordan, situated in a mountainous country*,
whither (according to Eusebius, who resided near the spot) they came from Jerusalem, and settled, before the war under
Vespasian began.   Other providential op-
portunities for escaping afterwards occurred, of which, it is probable, those who
were now left behind availed themselves;
for it is a striking fact, and as such cannot be contemplated by the pious mind
without sentiments of devout admiration,
that history does not record that even one
christian perished in the siege of Jerusalem.   Enduring to the end faithful to their

---

* Such was our Lord's admonition : " *Let them which
be in Judea flee into the mountains,*" &c.   *Vide* Mat. xxiv.
16—22.

blessed Master, they gave full credit to his predictions, and escaped the calamity Thus were fulfilled the words of our Lord, *" He that shall endure unto the end* (i. e. of the scene of this prophecy) *shall be saved*,"* i. e. from the calamities which will involve all those who shall continue obstinate in unbelief.

Nero, having been informed of the defeat of Cestius, immediately appointed Vespasian, a man of tried valour, to prosecute the war against the Jews, who, assisted by his son Titus, soon collected at Ptolemais an army of sixty thousand men. From hence, in the spring of 67 A. D. he marched into Judea, every where spreading the most cruel havoc and devastation : the Roman soldiers, on various occasions, sparing neither infants nor the aged. For fifteen months Vespasian proceeded in this sanguinary career, during which period he reduced all the strong towns of

---

* Mat. xxiv. 13.

Galilee, and the chief of those in Judea, destroying at least one hundred and fifty thousand of the inhabitants. Among the terrible calamities which at this time happened to the Jews, those which befel them at Joppa, which had been rebuilt, deserve particular notice. Their frequent piracies had provoked the vengeance of Vespasian. The Jews fled before his army to their ships; but a tempest immediately arose, and pursued such as stood out to sea, and overset them, while the rest were dashed vessel against vessel, and against the rocks, in the most tremendous manner. In this perplexity some were drowned, some were crushed by the broken ships, others killed themselves, and such as reached the shore were slain by the merciless Romans. The sea for a long space was stained with blood; four thousand two hundred dead bodies were strewed along the coast, and, dreadful to relate, not an individual survived to report this great calamity at Jerusalem. Such events were foretold by our Lord, when he said, " *There shall be distress of na-tions, with perplexity; the sea and the waves roaring*.*"

Vespasian, after proceeding as far as Jericho, returned to Cæsarea, in order to make preparations for his grand attempt against Jerusalem. While he was thus employed, he received intelligence of the death of Nero; whereupon, not knowing what the will of the future emperor might be, he prudently resolved to suspend, for the present, the execution of his design. Thus the Almighty gave the Jews a se-cond respite, which continued nearly two years; but they repented not of their crimes, neither were they in the least de-gree reclaimed, but rather proceeded to acts of still greater enormity. The flame of civil dissention again burst out, and with more dreadful fury. In the heart of Jerusalem two factions, contending for the sovereignty, raged against each other with

* Luke xxi. 25.

rancorous and destructive animosity. A division of one of these factions having been excluded from the city (*vide* page 34), forcibly entered it during the night. Athirst for blood, and inflamed by revenge, they spared neither age, sex, nor infancy ; and the morning sun beheld eight thousand five hundred dead bodies lying in the streets of the holy city. They plundered every house, and having found the chief priests, Ananus and Jesus, not only slew them, but, insulting their bodies, cast them forth unburied. They slaughtered the common people as unfeelingly as if they had been a herd of the vilest beasts. The nobles they first imprisoned, then scourged, and when they could not by these means attach them to their party, they bestowed death upon them as a favour. Of the higher classes twelve thousand perished in this manner ; nor did any one dare to shed a tear, or utter a groan, openly, through fear of a similar fate. Death, indeed, was the penalty of the lightest and heaviest accusation, nor did any escape through the meanness of their birth, or their poverty. Such as fled were intercepted and slain: their carcasses lay in heaps on all the public roads: every symptom of pity seemed utterly extinguished, and with it all respect for authority, both human and divine.

While Jerusalem was a prey to these ferocious and devouring factions, every part of Judea was scourged and laid waste by bands of robbers and murderers, who plundered the towns, and, in case of resistance, slew the inhabitants, not sparing either women or children. Simon, son of Gioras, the commander of one of these bands, at the head of forty thousand banditti, having with some difficulty entered Jerusalem, gave birth to a third faction, and the flame of civil discord blazed out again, with still more destructive fury. The three factions, rendered frantic by drunkenness, rage, and desperation, tramp-

F

ling on heaps of slain, fought against each other with brutal savageness and madness. Even such as brought sacrifices to the temple were murdered. The dead bodies of priests and worshippers, both natives and foreigners, were heaped together, and a lake of blood stagnated in the sacred courts. John of Gischala, who headed one of the factions, burnt store-houses full of provisions; and Simon, his great antagonist, who headed another of them, soon afterwards followed his example.— Thus they cut the very sinews of their own strength. At this critical and alarming conjuncture, intelligence arrived that the Roman army was approaching the city. The Jews were petrified with astonishment and fear; there was no time for counsel, no hope of pacification, no means of flight :—all was wild disorder and perplexity :—nothing was to be heard but " *the confused noise of the warrior,*"—nothing to be seen but " *garments rolled in blood,*"—nothing to be

expected from the Romans but signal
and exemplary vengeance. A ceaseless
cry of combatants was heard day and
night, and yet the lamentations of mourn-
ers were still more dreadful. The con-
sternation and terror which now prevailed,
induced many of the inhabitants to desire
that a foreign foe might come, and effect
their deliverance. Such was the horrible
condition of the place when Titus and his
army presented themselves, and encamped before Jerusalem ; but, alas ! not to deliver it from its miseries, but to fulfil the
prediction, and vindicate the benevolent
warning of our Lord : *" When ye see* (he
had said to his disciples) *the abomination of
desolation, spoken of by the prophet Daniel,
standing in the holy place**, and Jerusalem
surrounded by armies* (or camps), *then let
those who are in the midst of Jerusalem depart and let not those who are in the country*

---

* Not only was the temple and mountain on which it
stood accounted *holy*, but also the whole city of Jerusalem, and several furlongs of land round about it. *Vide*
Neh. xi. 1 ; Isaiah liii. 1 ; Daniel ix. 24 ; and Mat. xxvii. 53.

enter into her," for " *then know that the desolation thereof is nigh*.*"   These armies,
we do not hesitate to affirm, were those of
the Romans, who now invested the city.
From the time of the Babylonian captivity, idolatry had been held as an abomination by the Jews.   This national aversion
was manifested even against the images
of their gods and emperors, which the
Roman armies carried in their standards ;
so that, in a time of peace, Pilate, and afterwards Vitellius, at the request of some
eminent Jews, on this account avoided
marching their forces through Judea.   Of
the desolating disposition which now gov-
erned the Roman army, the history of the
Jewish war, and especially the final demolition of the holy city, presents an awful
and signal example.   Jerusalem was not
captured merely, but, with its celebrated
temple, laid in ruins.   Lest, however, the
army of Titus should not be sufficiently
designated by this expression, our Lord
adds, " *Wheresoever the carcase is, there*

---

* Mat. xxiv. 15, 21 ; Luke xxi. 20, 21.

will the eagles be gathered together*."
The Jewish state, indeed, at this time, was
fitly compared to a carcass. The sceptre
of Judah, i. e. its civil and political authority, the life of its religion, and the
glory of its temple, were departed. It
was, in short, morally and judicially dead.
The eagle, whose ruling instinct is rapine
and murder, as fitly represented the fierce
and sanguinary temper of the Romans,
and, perhaps, might be intended to refer
also to the principal figure on their ensigns, which, however obnoxious to the
Jews, were at length planted in the midst
of the holy city, and finally on the temple
itself.

The day on which Titus encompassed
Jerusalem was the feast of the passover;
and it is deserving of the very particular
attention of the reader, that this was the
anniversary of that memorable period in
which the Jews crucified their Messiah (

* Mat. xxiv. 28.

F 2

At this season multitudes came up from all the surrounding country, and from distant parts, to keep the festival. How suitable and how kind, then, was the prophetic admonition of our Lord, and how clearly he saw into futurity when he said, "*Let not them that are in the countries enter into Jerusalem*.*" Nevertheless, the city was at that time crowded with Jewish strangers, and foreigners from all parts, so that the whole nation may be considered as having been shut up in one prison, preparatory to the execution of the Divine vengeance; and, according to Josephus, this event took place suddenly; thus, not only fulfilling the predictions of our Lord, that these calamities should come like the swift darting lightning "*that cometh out of the east and shineth even unto the west,*" and "*as a snare on all them* (the Jews) *who dwelt upon the face of the whole earth*†;" but justifying, also, his friendly direction, that those who fled from the

---

* Luke xxi. 22. † Mat. xxiv. 27; and Luke xxi. 35.

place should use the utmost possible expedition.

On the appearance of the Roman army, the factious Jews united, and, rushing furiously out of the city, repulsed the tenth legion, which was with difficulty preserved. This event caused a short suspension of hostilities, and, by opening the gates, gave an opportunity to such as were so disposed to make their escape; which, before this, they could not have attempted without interruption, from the suspicion that they wished to revolt to the Romans. This success inspired the Jews with confidence, and they resolved to defend their city to the very uttermost; but it did not prevent the renewal of their civil broils. The faction under Eleazer having dispersed, and arranged themselves under the two other leaders, John and Simon, there ensued a scene of the most dreadful contention, plunder, and conflagration: the middle space of the city being burnt, and the wretched inhabitants made the prize of the contending parties. The Romans at length gained possession of two of the three walls which defended the city, and fear once more united the factions. This pause to their fury had, however, scarcely begun, when famine made its ghastly appearance in the Jewish army. It had for some time been silently approaching, and many of the peaceful and the poor had already perished for want of necessaries. With this new calamity, strange to relate, the madness of the factions again returned, and the city presented a new picture of wretchedness. Impelled by the cravings of hunger, they snatched the staff of life out of each other's hands, and many devoured the grain unprepared. Tortures were inflicted for the discovery of a handful of meal; women forced food from their husbands, and children from their fathers, and even mothers from their infants; and, while sucking children were wasting away in their arms, they scrupled not to take away the vital drops which sustained them! So justly did our Lord pronounce a wo on " *them who should give suck in those days*.*" This dreadful scourge at length drove multitudes of the Jews out of the city into the enemies' camp, where the Romans crucified them in such numbers, that, as Josephus relates, space was wanted for the crosses, and crosses for the captives ; and it having been discovered that some of them had swallowed gold, the Arabs and Syrians, who were incorporated in the Roman army, impelled by avarice, with unexampled cruelty, ripped open two thousand of the deserters in one night. Titus, touched by these calamities, in person entreated the Jews to surrender, but they answered him with revilings. Exasperated by their obstinacy and insolence, he now resolved to surround the city by a circumvallation†, which, with astonishing activity,

---

* Mat. xxiv. 19.

† This trench was thirty-nine furlongs in circuit, and strengthened with thirteen towers.

was effected by the soldiers in three days. Thus was fulfilled another of our Lord's predictions, for he had said, while addressing this devoted city, " *Thine enemies shall cast a trench about thee, and compass thee round about, and keep thee in on every side**." As no supplies whatever could now enter the walls, the famine rapidly extended itself, and, increasing in horror, devoured whole families. The tops of houses and the recesses of the city, were covered with the carcasses of women, children, and aged men. The young men appeared like spectres in the places of public resort, and fell down lifeless in the streets. The dead were too numerous to be interred, and many expired in the performance of this office. The public calamity was too great for lamentation. Silence, and, as it were, a black and deadly night overspread the city. But even such a scene could not awe the robbers; they spoiled the tombs,

---

* Luke xix. 43.

and stripped the dead of their grave-
clothes, with an unfeeling and wild laugh-
ter. They tried the edges of their swords
on their carcasses, and even on some that
were yet breathing; while Simon Gioras
chose this melancholy and awful period
to manifest the deep malignity and cruelty
of his nature, in the execution of the
High Priest Matthias, and his three sons,
whom he caused to be condemned as
favourers of the Romans. The father,
in consideration of his having opened
the city gates to Simon, begged that he
might be executed previously to his children; but the unfeeling tyrant gave orders that he should be dispatched in the
last place, and in his expiring moments
insultingly asked him, whether the Romans could then relieve him.

While the city was in this dismal situation, a Jew named Mannæus fled to Titus,
and informed him, that from the beginning of the siege (14th April) to the first

of July following, one hundred and fifteen thousand eight hundred and eighty dead bodies had been carried through one gate only, which he had guarded. This man had been appointed to pay the public allowance for carrying the bodies out, and was therefore obliged to register them. Soon after several respectable individuals deserted to the Romans, and assured Titus that the whole number of the poor who had been cast out at the different gates, was not less than six hundred thousand. The report of these calamities excited pity in the Romans, and in a particular manner affected Titus, who, while surveying the immense number of dead bodies which were piled up under the walls, raised his hands towards heaven, and, appealing to the Almighty, solemnly protested that he had not been the cause of these deplorable calamities; which, indeed, the Jews, by their unexampled wickedness, rebellion, and obstinacy, had brought down upon their own heads.

After this, Josephus, in the name of Titus, earnestly exhorted John and his adherents to surrender; but the insolent rebel returned nothing but reproaches and imprecations, declaring his firm persuasion that Jerusalem, as it was God's own city, could never be taken: thus literally fulfilling the declaration of Micah, that the Jews, in their extremity, notwithstanding their crimes, would presumptuously " *lean upon the Lord and say, ' Is not the Lord among us? none evil can come upon us'*.* "

Meanwhile the horrors of famine grew still more melancholy and afflictive. The Jews, for want of food, were at length compelled to eat their belts, their sandals, the skins of their shields, dried grass, and even the ordure of oxen. In the depth of this horrible extremity, a Jewess of noble family, urged by the intolerable cravings of hunger, slew her infant child, and prepared it for a meal; and had actually eat-

* Micah iii. 11.

G

en one half thereof, when the soldiers, al-
lured by the smell of food, threatened her
with instant death if she refused to discover it.   Intimidated by this menace, she
immediately produced the remains of her
son, which petrified them with horror.   At
the recital of this melancholy and affecting
occurrence, the whole city stood aghast,
and poured forth their congratulations on
those whom death had hurried away from
such heart-rending scenes.   Indeed, humanity at once shudders and sickens at
the narration, nor can any one of the least
sensibility reflect upon the pitiable condition to which the female part of the inhabitants of Jerusalem must at this time
have been reduced, without experiencing
the tenderest emotions of sympathy, or re-
frain from tears while he reads our Saviour's pathetic address to the women who
" *bewailed him*" as he was led to Calvary,
wherein he evidently refers to these very
calamities: " *Daughters of Jerusalem,
weep not for me, but for yourselves and for*

your children; for, behold, the days are coming in which they shall say, ' Blessed are the barren, and the wombs that never bear, and the breasts that never gave suck'*."

The above melancholy fact was also literally foretold by Moses: " *The tender and delicate woman among you* (said he, addressing Israel) *who would not venture to set the sole of her foot upon the ground for delicateness and tenderness, her eye shall be evil . . . toward her young one . . . which she shall bear,*" and " *eat for wan of all things, secretly, in the siege and straitness wherewith thine enemy shall distress thee in thy gates†.*" This prediction was partially fulfilled, when Samaria, the capital of the revolted tribes. was besieged by Benhadad; and afterwards at Jerusalem, previously to its capture by Nebuchadnezzar; but its exact and literal accomplishment, in relation to

---

* Luke xxiii. 29.   † Deut. xxviii. 56, 57.

a lady of rank, delicately and voluptuously educated, was reserved for the period of which we are now speaking. And it deserves particular regard, as a circumstance which very greatly enhances the importance of this prophecy, that the history of the world does not record that a parallel instance of unnatural barbarity ever occurred during the siege of any other place, in any other age or nation whatsoever. Indeed, Josephus himself declares that, if there had not been many credible witnesses of the fact, he would not have recorded it, " because," as he remarks, " such a shocking violation of nature never having been perpetrated by any Greek or barbarian," the insertion of it might have diminished the credibility of his history.

While famine continued thus to spread its destructive rage through the city, the Romans, after many ineffectual attempts, at length succeeded in demolishing part of

the inner wall, possessed themselves of
the great tower of Antonia, and advanced
towards the temple, which Titus, in a
council of war, had determined to preserve as an ornament to the empire, and as
a monument of his success; but the Almighty had determined otherwise; for
now, in the revolution of ages, was arriv
ed that fatal day*, emphatically called a
" *day of vengeance*†," on which the
temple had formerly been destroyed by
the king of Babylon. A Roman soldier,
urged, as he declared, by a divine im-
pulse, regardless of the command of Titus climbed on the shoulders of another,
and threw a flaming brand into the golden
window of the temple, which instantly set
the building on fire. The Jews, anxious
above all things to save that sacred edifice, in which they superstitiously trusted
for security, with a dreadful outcry, rushed in to extinguish the flames. Titus
also, being informed of the conflagration,

---

* The 10th of August.   † Luke xxi. 22.

G 2

hastened to the spot in his chariot, attend-
ed by his principal officers and legions ,
but in vain he waved his hand and raised
his voice, commanding his soldiers to extinguish the fire; so great was the uproar
and confusion, that no attention was paid
even to him.   The Romans, wilfully deaf,
instead of extinguishing the flames, spread
them wider and wider.   Actuated by the
fiercest impulses of rancour and revenge
against the Jews, they rushed furiously
upon them, slaying some with the sword,
trampling others under their feet, or
crushing them to death against the walls.
Many, falling amongst the smoking ruins
of the porches and galleries, were suffo-
cated.   The unarmed poor, and even sick
persons, were slaughtered without mercy.
Of these unhappy people numbers were
left weltering in their gore.   Multitudes
of the dead and dying were heaped round
about the altar, to which they had formerly fled for protection, while the steps that

led from it into the outer court were literally deluged with their blood.

Finding it impossible to restrain the
impetuosity and cruelty of his soldiers,
the commander in chief proceeded, with
some of his superior officers, to take a
survey of those parts of the edifice which
were still uninjured by the conflagration.
It had not, at this time, reached the inner
temple, which Titus entered, and viewed
with silent admiration. Struck with the
magnificence of its decorations, which even
surpassed the report of fame concerning
them ; and perceiving that the sanctuary
had not yet caught fire, he redoubled his
efforts to stop the progress of the flames.
He condescended even to intreat his soldiers to exert all their strength and activity for this purpose, and appointed a cen-
turion of the guards to punish them, if
they again disregarded him ; but all was
in vain. The delirious rage of the sol-

diery knew no bounds. Eager for plunder and for slaughter, they alike condemned the solicitations and the menaces of
their general. Even while he was thus
intent upon the preservation of the sanctuary, one of the soldiers was actually employed in setting fire to the door posts,
which caused the conflagration to become
general. Titus and his officers were now
compelled to retire, and none remained to
check the fury of the soldiers or the
flames. The Romans, exasperated to the
highest pitch against the Jews, seized
every person whom they could find, and,
without the least regard to sex, age, or
quality, first plundered, and then slew
them. The old and the young, the common people and the priests, those who
surrendered and those who resisted, were
equally involved in this horrible and indis-
criminate carnage. Meanwhile the temple continued burning, until at length,
vast as was its size, the flames completely
enveloped the whole building ; which,

from the extent of the conflagration, impressed the distant spectator with an idea that the whole city was now on fire. The tumult and disorder which ensued upon this event it is impossible (says Josephus) for language to describe. The Roman legions made the most horrid outcries; the rebels, finding themselves exposed to the fury of both fire and sword, screamed dreadfully; while the unhappy people who were pent up between the enemy and the flames, deplored their situation in the most pitiable complaints. Those on the hill and those in the city seemed mutually to return the groans of each other. Such as were expiring through famine, were revived by this scene, and seemed to acquire new spirits to deplore their misfortunes. The lamentations from the city were re-echoed from the adjacent mountains, and places beyond Jordan. The flames which enveloped the temple were so violent and impetuous, that the lofty hill on which it stood appeared, even from its deep foundation, as one large fire. The blood of the sufferers flowed in proportion to the rage of this destructive element; and the number of the slain exceeded all calculation. The ground could not be seen for the dead bodies, over which the Romans trampled in pursuit of the fugitives; while the crackling noise of the devouring flames, mingled with the clangour of arms, the groans of the dying, and the shrieks of despair, augmented the tremendous horror of a scene, to which the pages of history can furnish no parallel.

Amongst the tragical events which at this time occurred, the following is more particularly deserving of notice: a false prophet, pretending to a divine commission, affirmed, that if the people would repair to the temple, they should behold signs of their speedy deliverance. Accordingly, about six thousand persons, chiefly women and children, assembled

in a gallery, that was yet standing, on
the outside of the building. Whilst
they waited in anxious expectation of the
promised miracle, the Romans, with the
most wanton barbarity, set fire to the gallery; from which, multitudes, rendered
frantic by their horrible situation, precipi-
tated themselves on the ruins below, and
were killed by the fall; while, awful to
relate, the rest, without a single excep-
tion, perished in the flames. So necessary
was our Lord's second premonition not
to give credit to " *false prophets*," who
should pretend to show " *great signs and
wonders.*" In this last caution, as the
connection of the prophecy demonstrates,
he evidently refers to the period of the
siege, but, in the former, to the interval
immediately preceding the Jewish war*.

The temple now presented little more
than a heap of ruins; and the Roman
army, as in triumph on the event, came

* Mat. xxiv. Compare verses 5, and 23, 24, 25, 26.

and reared the ensigns against a fragment of the eastern gate, and, with sacrifices of thanksgiving, proclaimed the imperial majesty of Titus, with every possible demonstration of joy.

Thus terminated the glory and the existence of this sacred and venerable edifice, which, from its stupendous size, its massy solidity, and astonishing strength, seemed formed to resist the most violent operations of human force, and to stand, like the pyramids, amid the shocks of successive ages, until the final dissolution of the globe*.

* From its first foundation by king Solomon, until its destruction under Vespasian, were one thousand and thirty years, seven months, and fifteen days : and from its re-erection by Haggai, to the same period, six hundred and thirty-nine years, and forty-five days. It has been already hinted, that, by a very singular coincidence, it was now reduced to ashes in the same month and on the same day of the month, on which it had formerly been burnt by the Babylonians. These two eras are distinguished by another extraordinary coincidence, which Josephus, in one of his addresses to the Jews, pointed out to them as one of the signs which foreboded the destruction of their city. "The fountains," said he, "flow copiously for

For five days after the destruction of the temple, the priests who had escaped, sat, pining with hunger, on the top of one of its broken walls; at length, through necessity, they came down and humbly asked the pardon of Titus, which, however, he refused to grant them, saying, that, " as the temple, for the sake of which he would have spared them, was destroyed, it was but fit that its priests should perish also ;"—whereupon he commanded that they should be put to death.

The leaders of the factions being now pressed on all sides, begged a conference with Titus, who offered to spare their

Titus, which to you were dried up ; for before he came, you know that both Siloam failed, and all the springs without the city, so that water was brought by the amphora* ; but now they are so abundant to your enemies, as to suffice, not only for themselves and their cattle, but also for their gardens. This wonder you also formerly experienced when the king of Babylon laid siege to your city."

* *A vessel containing about seven gallons.*

lives, provided that they would lay down their arms. With this reasonable condition, however, they refused to comply; upon which Titus, exasperated by their obstinacy, resolved that he would hereafter grant no pardon to the insurgents, and ordered a proclamation to be made to this effect. The Romans had now full licence to ravage and destroy. Early the following morning they set fire to the castle, the register-office, the council-chamber, and the palace of queen Helena; and then spread themselves throughout the city, slaughtering wherever they came, and burning the dead bodies which were scattered over every street, and on the floors of almost every house. In the royal palace, where immense treasures were deposited, the seditious Jews murdered eight thousand four hundred of their own nation, and afterwards plundered their property. Prodigious numbers of deserters, also, who escaped from the tyrants, and fled into the enemies' camp, were slain. The

soldiers, however, at length, weary of
killing, and satiated with the blood which
they had spilt, laid down their swords, and
sought to gratify their avarice.   For this
purpose they took the Jews, together with
their wives and families, and publicly sold
them like cattle in a market, but at a very
low price; for multitudes were exposed
to sale, while the purchasers were few in
number.   And now were fulfilled the
words of Moses: "*And ye shall be sold*
for bond-men and bond-women, and no man
shall buy you*."

The Romans having become masters of
the lower city, set it on fire.   The Jews
now fled to the higher, from whence, their
pride and insolence yet unabated, they
continued to exasperate their enemies, and
even appeared to view the burning of the
town below them with tokens of pleasure.
In a short time, however, the walls of the
higher city were demolished by the Ro-

* Deut. xxviii. 68.

man engines, and the Jews, lately so
haughty and presumptuous, now, trem-
bling and panic-struck, fell on their faces,
and deplored their own infatuation.   Such
as were in the towers deemed impregnable to human force, beyond measure affrighted, strangely forsook them, and
sought refuge in caverns and subterrane-
ous passages; in which dismal retreats no
less than two thousand dead bodies were
afterwards found.   Thus, as our Lord
had predicted, did these miserable crea-
tures, in effect, say, "*to the mountains,*
'Fall on us;' and to the rocks, 'Cover
us**.*"

The walls of the city being now completely in possession of the Romans, they
hoisted their colours upon the towers, and
burst forth into the most triumphant acclamations.   After this, all annoyance from
the Jews being at an end, the soldiers
gave an unbridled license to their fury
against the inhabitants.   They first plun-

---

* Luke xxiii. 20.

dered, and then set fire to the houses.
They ranged through the streets with
drawn swords in their hands, murdering
every Jew whom they met without distinction; until, at length, the bodies of the
dead choaked up all the alleys and narrow
passes, while their blood literally flowed
down the channels of the city in streams.
As it drew towards evening, the soldiers
exchanged the sword for the torch, and
amidst the darkness of this awful night, set
fire to the remaining divisions of the place.
The vial of divine wrath which had been
so long pouring out upon this devoted
city, was now emptying, and Jerusalem,
once "a praise in all the earth," and the
subject of a thousand prophecies, deprived
of the staff of life, wrapt in flames, and
bleeding on every side, sunk into utter
ruin and desolation*.

---

* This memorable siege terminated on the 8th day of
September, A. D. 70: its duration was nearly five months,
the Romans having invested the city on the 14th day of
the preceding April.

Before their final demolition, however, Titus took a survey of the city and its fortifications; and, while contemplating their impregnable strength, could not help ascribing his success to the peculiar interposition of the Almighty himself. "Had not God himself (exclaimed he) aided our operations, and driven the Jews from their fortresses, it would have been absolutely impossible to have taken them; for what could men and the force of engines, have done against such towers as these?" After this he commanded that the city should be razed to its foundations, excepting only the three lofty towers, Hippocos, Phasael, and Marianne, which he suffered to remain as evidences of its strength, and as trophies of his victory. There was left standing, also, a small part of the western wall, as a rampart for a garrison, to keep the surrounding country in subjection. Titus now gave orders that those Jews only who resisted should be slain;

but the soldiers, equally void of pity and remorse, slew even the sick and the aged. The robbers and seditious were all punished with death : the tallest and most beautiful youths, together with several of the Jewish nobles, were reserved by Titus to grace his triumphal entry into Rome. After this selection, all above the age of seventeen were sent in chains into Egypt, to be employed there as slaves, or distributed throughout the empire, to be sacrificed as gladiators in the amphitheatres; whilst those who were under this age, were exposed to sale.

During the time that these things were transacting, eleven thousand Jews, guarded by one of the generals, named Fronto, were literally starved to death. This melancholy occurrence happened partly through the scarcity of provisions, and partly through their own obstinacy, and the negligence of the Romans.

Of the Jews destroyed during the siege, Josephus reckons not less than one million and one hundred thousand, to which must be added, above two hundred and thirty-seven thousand who perish*ed in other places, and innumerable multitudes who were swept away by famine and pestilence, and of which no calculation could be made. Not less than two thousand laid violent hands upon themselves. Of the captives, the whole number was about ninety-seven thousand. Of the two great leaders of the Jews, who had both been made prisoners, John was doomed to a dungeon for life; while Simon, after being led, together with John, in triumph at Rome, was scourged, and put to death as a malefactor.

In executing the command of Titus, relative to the demolition of Jerusalem, the Roman soldiers not only threw down the buildings, but even dug up their foundations, and so completely levelled the whole circuit of the city, that a stranger would scarcely have known that it had ever been inhabited by human beings. Thus was this great city, which, only five months before, had been crowded with nearly two millions of people, who gloried in its impregnable strength, entirely depopulated, and levelled with the ground. And thus, also, was our Lord's prediction, that her enemies should *" lay her even with the ground,"* and *" should not leave in her one stone upon another*,"* most strikingly and fully accomplished !—— This fact is confirmed by Eusebius, who asserts that he himself saw the city lying in ruins; and Josephus introduces Eleazer as exclaiming, " Where is our great city, which, it was believed, God inhabited? It is altogether rooted and torn up from its foundations; and the only monument of it that remains, is the camp of its destroyers, pitched amidst its reliques!"

---

* Luke xix. 44.

Concerning the temple, our Lord had foretold, particularly, that notwithstanding their wonderful dimensions, there should *" not be left one stone upon another that should not be thrown down ;"* and, accordingly, it is recorded in the Talmud, and by Maimonides, that Terentius Rufus, captain of the army of Titus, absolutely ploughed up the foundations of the temple with a ploughshare. Now, also, was literally fulfilled that prophecy of Micah,—*" Therefore shall Zion, for your sakes* (i. e. for your wickedness), *be ploughed as a field, and Jerusalem shall become heaps, and the mountain of the Lord's house as the high places of the forest*."*

Thus awfully complete, and severe beyond example, were the calamities which befel the Jewish nation, and especially the city of Jerusalem. With what truth, then, did our Lord declare, that there should

---

* Mic. iii. 12.

" be great tribulation, such as was not since the beginning of the world, no, nor never shall be*!" Such was the prediction: the language in which Josephus declares its fulfilment is an exact counterpart to it: "If the misfortunes," says he, "of all nations, from the beginning of the world, were compared with those which befel the Jews, they would appear far less in comparison;" and again, "No other city ever suffered such things, as no other generation, from the beginning of the world, was ever more fruitful in wickedness." These were, indeed, *" the days of vengeance," " that all things which are written* (especially by Moses, Joel, and Daniel) *might be fulfilled†."* Nor were the calamities of this ill-fated nation even now ended; for there were still other places to subdue; and our Lord had thus predicted, *" wheresoever the carcase is, there will the eagles be gathered together‡."* After the destruction

---

* Mat. xxiv. 21.   † Luke xxi. 22.   ‡ Mat. xxiv. 28.

of Jerusalem seventeen hundred Jews who surrendered at Macherus were slain, and of fugitives not less than three thousand in the wood of Jardes. Titus having marched his army to Cæsarea, he there, with great splendour, celebrated the birthday of his brother Domitian; and, according to the barbarous manner of those times, punished many Jews in honour of it. The number who were burnt, and who fell by fighting with wild beasts, and in mutual combats, exceeded two thousand and five hundred. At the siege of Massada, Eleazer, the commander, instigated the garrison to burn their stores, and to destroy first the women and children, and then themselves. Dreadful as it is to relate, this horrid design was executed. They were in number nine hundred and sixty. Ten were chosen to perform this bloody work: the rest sat on the ground, and, embracing their wives and children, stretched out their necks to the sword: one was afterwards appointed to destroy

the remaining nine, and then himself. The
survivor, when he had looked round to
see that all were slain, set fire to the place,
and plunged his sword into his own bo-
som. Nevertheless, two women and five
children successfully concealed themselves, and witnessed the whole transaction. When the Romans advanced to the
attack in the morning, one of the women
gave them a distinct account of this melancholy affair ; which struck them with
amazement at the contempt of death that
had been displayed by the Jews. After
this event, if we except the transitory in-
surrection of the Sicarii, under Jonathan,
all opposition on the part of the Jews
every where ceased. It was the submission of impotence and despair. The
peace that ensued was the effect of the
direst necessity. The rich territory of
Judea was converted into a desolate waste.
Every where ruin and desolation presented itself to the solitary passenger, and a
melancholy and death-like silence reigned

over the whole region.   The mournful
and desolate condition of Judea, at this
time, is exactly described by the prophet
Isaiah, in the following passage of his prophecy : " *The cities were wasted without
inhabitant, and the houses without a man,
and the land was utterly desolate, and the
Lord had removed men far away, and
there was a great forsaking in the midst of
the land*.*"

The catastrophe which has now been
reviewed, cannot but be deemed one of
the most extraordinary that has happened
since the foundation of the world; and as
it has pleased the Almighty to make it the
subject of a very large proportion of the
prophecies, both of the Jewish and christian scriptures, so he hath ordained that
the particular events which accomplished
them, should be recorded with very remarkable precision, and by a man most

---

* Isaiah vi. 11, 12.

singularly preserved*, qualified, and circumstanced for this purpose. But with respect to this latter point, he shall speak for himself: "At first," says Josephus, "I fought against the Romans, but was afterwards forced to be present in the Roman camp. At the time I surrendered, Vespasian and Titus kept me in bonds, but obliged me to attend them continually. Afterwards I was set at liberty, and accompanied Titus when he came from Alexandria to the siege of Jerusalem.— During this time nothing was done which escaped my knowledge. What happened in the Roman camp I saw, and wrote down carefully. As to the information the deserters brought out of the city, I was the only man that understood it. Afterwards I got leisure at Rome; and when all my materials were prepared, I procured the help of one to assist me in writing Greek. Thus I composed the

* Three several times his life was preserved as by a miracle.

history of those transactions, and I appeal both to Titus and Vespasian for the truth of it; to which also Julius Archelaus, Herod, and King Aggrippa, bore their testimony." All remark here is needless; but it should not be forgotten, that Josephus was a Jew, obstinately attached to his religion; and that, although he has circumstantially related every remarkable event of that period, he seems studiously to have avoided such as had any reference to Jesus Christ, whose history (and even the genuineness of this is disputed) he sums up in about twelve lines. No one, therefore, can reasonably entertain a suspicion, that the service he has rendered to christianity, by his narrative of the transactions of the Jewish war, was at all the effect of design. The fidelity of Josephus, as an historian, is, indeed, universally admitted; and Scaliger even affirms, that, not only in the affairs of the Jews, but in those of foreign nations also, he deserves more credit than all the Greek and Roman writers put together.

Nor is the peculiar character of Titus, the chief commander in this war, unworthy of our particular regard. Vespasian his father, had risen out of obscurity, and was elected emperor, contrary to his avowed inclination, about the commencement of the conflict; and thus the chief command devolved upon Titus, the most unlikely man throughout the Roman armies to become a scourge to Jerusalem. He was eminently distinguished for his great tenderness and humanity, which he displayed in a variety of instances during the siege. He repeatedly made pacific overtures to the Jews, and deeply lamented the infatuation that rejected them. In short, he did every thing, which a military commander could do, to spare them, and to preserve their city and temple, but without effect. Thus was the will of God accomplished by the agency, although contrary to the wish of Titus; and his predicted interposition, to punish his rebellious and apostate people, in this way rendered more conspicuously evident.

The history of the Jews, subsequently to the time of Josephus, still further corroborates the truth of our Saviour's prophecies concerning that oppressed and persecuted people. Into this inquiry, however, the limits of the present essay will not allow us to enter particularly. Our Lord foretold, generally, that they should " *fall by the edge of the sword, and be led away captive into all nations; and that Jerusalem should be trodden down of the Gentiles, until the time of the Gentiles should be fulfilled*;" and these predictions may be regarded as a faithful epitome of the circumstances of the Jews, and also of their city, from the period in which it was delivered, down even to our own times.

---

* Luke xxi. 24.

In order to demonstrate the accomplishment of these predictions, we appeal, therefore, to universal history, and to every country under heaven*. The un-

---

* " In the reign of Adrian," says Bishop Newton, " nine hundred and eighty-five of their best towns were sacked and demolished, five hundred and eighty thou sand men fell by the sword, in battle, besides an infinite multitude who perished by famine, and sickness, and fire, so that Judea was depopulated, and an almost incredible number, of every age and of each sex, were sold like horses, and dispersed over the face of the earth*." The war which gave rise to these calamities, happened about sixty-four years after the destruction of Jerusalem; dur ing which time the Jews had greatly multiplied in Ju dea. About fifty years after the latter event, Ælius Ad rian built a new city on Mount Calvary, and called i Ælia, after his own name; but no Jew was suffered to come near it. He placed in it a heathen colony, and erected a temple to Jupiter Capitolinus, on the ruins of the temple of Jehovah. This event contributed greatly to provoke the sanguinary war to which we have just al luded. The Jews afterwards burnt the new city; which Adrian, however, re-built, and re-established the colony. In contempt of the Jews, he ordered a marble statue of a sow to be placed over its principal gate, and prohibited them entering the city under pain of death, and forbad them even to look at it from a distance. He also ordered fairs to be held annually for the sale of captive Jews, and banished such as dwelt in Canaan into Egypt. Constan-

* *Newton*, vol. ii. *Diss.* xviii.

disputed facts are, that Jerusalem has not
since been in possession of the Jews, but
has been successively occupied by the
Romans, Arabic Saracens, Franks, Mame-
lucs, and lastly by the Turks, who now
possess it. It has never regained its
former distinction and prosperity. It has
always been trodden down. The eagles
of idolatrous Rome, the crescent of Ma-
homet, and the banner of popery, have

---

tine greatly improved the city, and restored to it the name
of Jerusalem; but still he did not permit the Jews to
dwell there. To punish an attempt to recover the possession of their capital, he ordered their ears to be cut off,
their bodies to be marked as rebels, and dispersed them
through all the provinces of the empire as vagabonds and
slaves. Jovian having revived the severe edicts of Adrian,
which Julian had suspended, the wretched Jews even
bribed the soldiers with money, for the privilege only of
beholding the sacred ruins of their city and temple, and
weeping over them, which they were peculiarly solicit-
ous to do on the anniversary of that memorable day, on
which they were taken and destroyed by the Romans.
In short, during every successive age, and in all nations,
this ill-fated people have been constantly persecuted, en-
slaved, contemned, harassed, and oppressed; banished
from one country to another, and abused in all; while
countless multitudes have, at different periods, been barbarously massacred, particularly in Persia, Syria, Pales-
tine, and Egypt; and in Germany, Hungary, France, and
Spain.

by turns been displayed amidst the ruins of the sanctuary; and a Mahomedan mosque, to the extent of a mile in circumference, now covers ° the spot where the temple formerly stood. The territory of Judea, then one of the most fertile countries on the globe, has for more than seventeen hundred years continued a desolate waste. The Jews themselves, still miraculously preserved a distinct people, are, as we see, scattered over the whole earth, invigorating the faith of the Christian, flashing conviction in the face of the infidel, and constituting a universal, permanent, and invincible evidence of the truth of christianity.

In order to invalidate this evidence, the apostate emperor Julian, impelled by a spirit of enmity against the Christians, about A. D. 363, made an attempt to rebuild the city and temple of Jerusalem, and to recal the Jews to their own country. He assigned immense sums for the execution

of this great design, and commanded
Alypius of Antioch (who had formerly
served as a lieutenant in Britain) to super-
intend the work, and the governor of the
province to assist him therein. "But,"
says Ammianus Marcellinus, "whilst
they urged with vigour and diligence the
execution of the work, horrible balls of
fire, breaking out near the foundation,
with frequent and reiterated attacks, rendered the place, from time to time, inaccessible to the scorched and blasted work-
men; and the victorious element continuing, in this manner, obstinately and reso-
lutely bent, as it were, to drive them to
a distance, the undertaking was abandon-
ed." Speaking of this event, even Gibbon, who is notorious for his scepticism,
acknowledges, that "an earthquake, a
whirlwind, and a fiery eruption, which
overturned and scattered the new foundations of the temple, are attested, with
some variations, by contemporary and
respectable evidence, by Ambrose, bishop

of Milan, Chrysostom, and Gregory Na-
zianzen, the latter of whom published his
account before the expiration of the same
year*." To these may be added the
names of Zemuch David, a Jew, who con-
fesses that " Julian was hindered by God
in the attempt;" of Rufinus, a Latin, of
T. eodoret and Sozomen among the or-
thodox, of Philostorgius, an Arian, and of
Socrates, a favourer of the Novatians, who
all recorded the same wonderful interposition of Providence, while the eye-wit-
nesses of the fact were yet living. The
words of Sozomen to this purport are remarkable: " If it yet seem incredible,"
says he, " to any one, he may repair both
to witnesses of it yet living, and to them
who have heard it from their mouths; yea,
they may view the foundations, lying yet
bare and naked." Besides, it may be added, that no other reason has ever been alleged, why Julian should abandon his magnificent but impious design.

---

* Decline and Fall, vol. iv. 8vo. page 107.

Thus was this celebrated emperor " taken in his own craftiness," and his presumptuous attempt to frustrate the plans,
and falsify the declarations of infinite om-
nipotence and wisdom, converted into a
new and striking evidence of their certainty
and truth*.

We shall now proceed to reply to two
or three objections, which may be rashly
opposed to the impregnable argument which
the preceding account furnishes in defence
of our religion.

I. It may be alleged, that the prophecies,
whose fulfilment has been demonstrated,
were not written until after the events to
which they refer were past.

Assertion is not proof; and even a conjecture to this effect, in the face of the his-

---

* This subject is discussed at length, with singular in-
genuity and force of argument, by the learned bishop
Warburton, in his work entitled Julian.

toric testimony, and general sentiment of seventeen ages, would be ridiculous. On the faith, then, of all antiquity, we affirm, that the gospels containing these predictions were written before the destruction of Jerusalem, and we confirm this assertion by particular proof. The gospel of St. Matthew, who died previously to that event, supposed to have been written about eight years after the ascension of our Saviour, was published before the dispersion of the apostles; for Eusebius says, that St. Bartholomew took a copy of it with him to India; and the dispersion of the apostles took place within twelve years after the ascension of our Lord. Mark must have written his gospel at the latest in the time of Nero, for he died in the eighth year of that emperor's reign. The gospel by St. Luke was written before the Acts, as the first verses of that narrative prove; and the Acts were written before the death of St. Paul, for they carry down his history only to A. D. 63; whereas he was not crucified until the 12th of Nero,

K

the very year before the Jewish war commenced.   Of Luke's death the time is un-
certain.   As to the Evangelist John, he
both lived and wrote after the destruction
of Jerusalem ; but then, as if purposely to
prevent this very cavil, his gospel does
not record the proph ics which foretold
it ! Learned men, indeed, differ with regard to the precise year in which the Evan-
gelists Matthew, Mark, and Luke wrote
their respective gospels; but they universally agree, that they were both written
and published before the destruction of
Jerusalem.   As to the gospel by St. John,
some are of opinion that it was written
before, and some after that event.

II. If it be objected, that, although the
gospel narratives might be written and
published before the destruction of Jerusalem, yet that the predictions relating to
that event may be subsequent interpola-
tions; we reply, that this cannot but be
considered as a preposterous supposition,
because those predictions are not confined

to the particular chapters to which we
have chiefly referred, but are closely and
inseparably interwoven with the general
texture of the history—because the character of the style is uniform—because
there is no allusion, in conformity to the
practice of the sacred historians*, to the
fulfilment of these prophecies—because
such an attempt must have destroyed the
cause it professed to serve, and, lastly, because " no unbeliever of the primitive
times (whether Jew or Gentile), when
pressed, as both frequently were, by this
prophecy, appear to have had recourse to
the charge of forgery or interpolation."
It may be added also, that, in modern
times, no distinguished unbeliever (not
even the arch-infidels Voltaire and Gibbon)
has had the temerity so much as to insinu-
ate a charge of this nature.

III. It may be alleged, that the accom-
plishments of our Lord's predictions relative to the destruction of Jerusalem, ought

---

* *Vide*, particularly, Acts xi. 28.

not to be deemed supernatural, inasmuch as the distresses of all great cities, during a siege, are similar, and because it is probable that, some time or other, such should be the fate of every city of this description; and that, since the obstinacy of the Jews was great, and their fortifications were strong, when war did come, Jerusalem was more likely to suffer under that form of it than any other.

In answer to this objection we remark, that it was not merely foretold that Jerusalem was to be destroyed, but that it was to be destroyed by the Romans; and so it was. But was this then a likely event? When our Lord delivered his predictions, Judea was already completely in their hands. Was it a probable thing that it should be desolated by its own masters? Or was it a natural thing that they should be indifferent to the revenue which was derived from a country so populous and fertile? Again, was it likely that this petty province should provoke the wrath and defy the power, of the universal empire? Or was it to be supposed that the mistress of the world, irresistible to all nations, instead of controuling, should deem it worthy of her utterly to exterminate a state comparatively so insignificant? Or did it accord with the disposition or custom of the Romans, like Goths, to demolish buildings famed for their antiquity and magnificence? Rather was it not to have been expected that they would preserve them, to maintain the renown and glory of their empire? Nevertheless, as we have seen, they did destroy them, and even the illustrious temple of Jerusalem, the chief ornament of Asia, and the wonder of the world. But it was predicted that " *thus it must be ;* " and therefore Titus himself, with all his authority and exertions, could not preserve it.

But there are a number of very material circumstances closely interwoven with the prophecy, that still further identify the events which fulfilled it, and demonstrate that the prophecy itself was something very different from a happy conjecture, suggested by the aspect of the times, or conclusions from past experience. For,

1. Our Lord foretold, as " *the begin-ning of sorrows*," and as alarming harbingers of his " *coming*," as " *the Son of Man*," to destroy Jerusalem, that terrible calamities would prevail in various parts of the world, during the intermediate period : and, unquestionably, this was the case. But it is very material to remark here, that our Lord did not describe these calamities in general terms merely, as an impostor might have done, but distinctly specified them thus : rumours of wars—actual wars—nation rising against nation —kingdom rising against kingdom—famines—pestilences—and eart; quakes, in divers places : which all came to pass accordingly, and nearly in the very order in which they were foretold. False prophets, also, were not merely to arise—but to personate the Messiah, to pretend to mi-

raculous powers, and to deceive many
and such were the characters and success
of those which actually appeared. Again,
the prognostics are not described as
" *sights*" merely, but as " *fearful sights;*"
not generally, as " *signs*," but as " *grea*
signs from heaven;" and such they were.
These wonderful appearances stand las
in the prophecy, and they occurred, according to Josephus, on the very eve of
the Jewish war*.

2. The investment of Jerusalem was to
take place " *suddenly*," " *as a snare*," which
predictions, as we have seen, were accomplished in the most surprising and extraordinary manner.

3. Our Lord declared also, that, " *except*
those days (i e. the " *days of vengeance*")
should be shortened, there should no flesh
be saved; but for the elect's† *sake* (said

---

* Vide page 34—40.

† i. e for the " sake" of the christians, who, no doubt
prayed ardently for the termination of these calamities.

he) *those days shall be shortened.*"—And
they were shortened accordingly: 1st, by
the determination of Titus vigorously to
push the siege by assault, in opposition to
the opinions of his officers, who recom-
mended the more tedious plan of block
ade: 2dly, by the conduct of the Jews
themselves, who accelerated the capture
of their city by intestine divisions and
mutual slaughters, contrary to what is
usual upon such emergencies, in which a
common sense of danger ordinarily tends
to unite contending parties against the
common foe: 3dly, by the madness of the
factions in burning storehouses full of
provisions, and thus wasting the strength
which was necessary for the defence of the
place: 4thly, by the extraordinary panic
by which the Jews were seized when the
Romans made their final attack on the
higher city, in consequence of which they
fled affrighted out of their strong holds,
which Titus afterwards pronounced to be
impregnable: and, lastly, by the crowded
state of the city during the siege, which,

as we have before remarked, occasioned pestilential disorders, and hastened the approach of famine.

4. Our Lord likewise foretold that his followers should escape the destruction of Jerusalem; and, accordingly, whilst countless multitudes of unbelieving Jews were fatally involved in this calamity, not a single christian perished therein; for he that " *knoweth how to deliver the godly out of temptations, and to reserve the unjust unto the day of judgment to be punished**," had said, that " *not a hair of their heads should perish*†." Who, that seriously meditates on these equitable arrangements of Providence, can help exclaiming, with the devout psalmist— " *Verily, there is a reward for the righteous; verily, he is a God that judgeth in the earth!*"

5. Our Lord declared also that the extreme miseries of the Jews should be

---

* 2 Peter ii. 9. † Luke xxi. 18.

without a parallel: and they certainly were, as Josephus himself repeatedly testifies, and as his history abundantly proves.

6. Again, our Lord foretold, that before the destruction of Jerusalem, the "*gospel should be preached in all the world as a witness unto all nations.*" This prediction, as we have seen already, was fully accomplished also; and yet, considering the character and condition of the instruments, the nature of the truths which they promulgated, the 'malignant opposition of their own countrymen, and the contempt with which, as Jews, they were regarded by the Gentile nations—nothing could scarcely have been •conceived less probable than such an event.

7. Our Lord further predicted, that the then existing generation should not "*pass away before all these things were fulfilled**;*" and, in conformity hereto, they were fulfilled within forty years from the

* Mat. xxiv. 34.

date of the prophecy. This is a very different thing from their being accomplished some time or other. Our Lord had intimated also, that the Evangelist John should survive the destruction of Jerusalem; and he survived it, accordingly, more than twenty-five years, and died at Ephesus nearly one hundred years old. How it came to pass that he who foresaw the persecutions of his disciples, and was therefore sensible of the dangers to which their lives would be exposed, should venture to predict that one of the most distinguished and zealous among them should escape martyrdom, and demonstrate, so long after the accomplishment of the prophecy, that the generation to which he addressed it had not even then " *passed away?*"

Now, if the destruction of Jerusalem were a subject of human conjecture merely, how came so great a variety of remarkable and improbable circumstances, as we have enumerated, to be unnecessarily interwoven with the prophecy? And how happened it that, in relation to those circumstances, as well as all others, of which the number is not small, the prophecy should be exactly fulfilled?

IV. If this prophecy be ascribed to political sagacity, we would ask, on the supposition of the infidel, how it happened that a carpenter's son, living nearly the whole of his life in privacy, associating chiefly with the poor, without access to the councils of princes, or to the society of the great, should possess a degree of political discernment to which no statesman would deem it less than folly to lay claim? Besides, how came he to predict the ruin of his own country, and at that very season, too, when all his countrymen turned their eyes to a deliverer, who should restore its sovereignty, consolidate its power, and extend both its boundaries and its renown? And, lastly, how came he even to conceive, much more cherish, such an idea, diametrically contrary as it was to all

his stubborn and deep-rooted prejudices as
a Jew?

Thus we perceive that the very objections which infidelity opposes to our argument, instead of invalidating, tend only
more fully to illustrate and confirm it.
And such, indeed, must always be the
happy effects of that hostility which is
directed against the evidences of the christian faith, since, the more carefully and attentively we examine the foundations
upon which it rests, the more perfectly
must we be convinced of the immovable
stability of the superstructure. Of that
evidence the prophecy which we have reviewed most certainly constitutes a very
striking and prominent part; from every
light and position in which it can be contemplated it constantly derives new lustre
and effect; and it may safely be considered
" as an unquestionable proof of the divine
foreknowledge of our Lord, and the divine
authority of the gospel: and on this
ground only, were it necessary, we might

securely rest the whole fabrick of our religion. Indeed, this remarkable prediction has always been considered, by every
impartial person, as one of the most powerful arguments in favour of christianity ;
and in our own times, more particularly,
a man of distinguished talents, and acknowledged eminence in his profession,
and in the constant habit of weighing,
sifting, and scrutinizing evidence with the
minutest accuracy in courts of justice, has
publicly declared, that he considered this
prophecy, if there were nothing else to
support christianity, as absolutely irresistible*."

Let us, then, if we are christians indeed,
offer up our grateful acknowledgments to
the Almighty, who hath laid such firm
foundations for our faith. Let us exult
in the inviolable certainty of his holy word,
and assure ourselves that his promises are

---

* See the Bishop of London's " Lectures on the Gospel of St. Matthew ;" and Mr. Erskine's eloquent speech
at the trial of Williams, for publishing Paine's Age of
Reason.

as infallible as his predictions: to "*the witness**" within us, and to an acquaintance with the interior excellence of the gospel, let us labour to add a more perfect knowledge of the historical and moral evidence which defends it; that thus we may be better qualified to convince gainsayers. More particularly, let us attend to that "*sure word of prophecy, whereunto we shall do well to take heed, as unto a light that shineth in a dark place†.*"

If we are christians in name only, let us receive a salutary admonition from that exemplary vengeance which was inflicted by the Almighty upon the whole Jewish nation; who, while "*they professed that they knew God, in works denied him;*" and while they boasted that they were his peculiar people, remained "*strangers to the covenant of promise.*" Let us also seriously reflect, that, as then he was not a Jew who was only one "*outwardly,*" "*in the letter*" merely, and whose praise was of

---

*1 John v. 10.   †2 Peter i. 19.

men—so now, in like manner, he only is a christian who is one "*inwardly*," whose religion is seated in the heart; "*in the spirit and not in the letter; whose praise is not of men but of God*.*"

Let the unbeliever, for whose benefit, chiefly, the preceding pages were written, seriously ponder their contents. Should the evidence which they contain in favour of christianity fail to convince him of its divine origin, it may be important for him to ask himself the following questions: "Can I reasonably require, for that purpose, stronger moral evidence than 'this? Can I conceive it possible that stronger evidence of this kind should be afforded? Am I capable of forming a scheme, of historical and moral proof, which shall not be liable to greater and more numerous objections? If I imagine myself equal to a task, at once so comprehensive and profound, have I also the resolution to enter upon it, to publish the scheme,

* Romans ii. 28, 29.

which I shall construct, for the decision of the world, and to stake the credit of my infidelity upon it?"

But it may be proper to inform the deist, that the faith which we wish him to possess is not merely an admission upon evidence, that *" all scripture is given by inspiration of God"* (which, standing alone, has no higher moral value than the faith of education which he ridicules), but a vital, active principle, a faith that will *"purify his heart;"* that *" works by love;"* that will enable him to *"fight the good fight,"* *" to overcome the world,"* and to obtain *" a crown of life,"* and *" an incorruptible inheritance"* in heaven*. It may be proper also to remind the unbeliever, that the evidence which has been adduced constitutes one only of those numerous bulwarks, more impregnable than the towers of Jerusalem, which encompass and defend christianity. But if this be the fact

---

* Acts xv. 9; Gal v. 6; 2 Tim. iv. 7; 1 John v. 4, 5; James i. 3, 12; 1 Peter i. 4, 5.

L 2

—and is it not? how great must be his temerity! how hopeless his warfare! how certain his defeat!

To the Jew we would say—Suspend, if it be practicable, the prejudices which you inherit from your forefathers, whilst you ponder, for one hour, the important and interesting subject of these pages—to you peculiarly interesting and important. Is it possible that you can attentively reflect upon the destruction of "the beloved city," the dispersion of your nation into all countries—the terrible calamities which have every where pursued them, for nearly 1800 years, even unto this day—and not trace therein the condign and predicted punishment of their original rejection, and continued contempt of that very Messiah whose character your own scriptures so faithfully pourtray*, and whose advent, precisely at the time of his actual appearance, they as clearly foretold† ? But your ancestors did not only reject,

* Isaiah iii. 53.   † Dan. ix. 26, 27.

ADDRESS TO THE JEW.   127

they also slew their Saviour. "*His blood*," said they, when calling upon Pilate to crucify him, "*his blood be on us and upon our children*." "A most fatal imprecation, and most dreadfully fulfilled upon them at the siege of Jerusalem, when the vengeance of heaven overtook them with a fury unexampled in the history of the world; when they were exposed at once to the horrors of famine, of sedition, of assassination, and the sword of the Romans *." Observe, too, the striking correspondence which marked their crimes in their punishment: "They put Jesus to death when the nation was assembled to celebrate the passover; and when the nation was assembled for the same purpose, Titus shut them up within the walls of Jerusalem †. The rejection of the Messiah was their crime, and the following of false Messiahs to their destruction was their punishment ‡.

---

* See the Bishop of London's Lectures, vol. ii. page 284; and Bishop Newton on the Prophecies, Diss. 21.
† Page 63 of this Treatise.   ‡ Ibid. 22.

They bought Jesus as a slave; and they themselves were afterwards sold and bought as slaves at the lowest prices* : they preferred a robber and a murderer to Jesus, whom they crucified between two thieves; and they themselves were after- wards infested with bands of thieves and robbers† : they put Jesus to death, lest the Romans should come and take away their place and nation; and the Romans did come and take away their place and nation‡ ; and what is still more striking, and still more strongly marks the judgment of God upon them, they were punished with that very kind of death which they were so eager to inflict on the Saviour of mankind, the death of the cross; and that in such pro- digious numbers, that Josephus assures us, there wanted wood for crosses, and room to place them in§.

---

* Ibid. 19.   † Ibid. 57.

‡ See page 59 of this Treatise.

§ See the Bishop of London's Lectures, and Bishop Newton, as before quoted; and this Treatise, page 63.

Now, according to your own scriptures, that fatal catastrophe which involved your ancestors in all these miseries, was not to take place until after the coming and crucifixion of their Messiah: for thus spake the prophet Daniel, prophesying almost five hundred and forty years before the birth of the Messiah: " *Know and under- stand, that from the going forth of the commandment to restore and to build Jeru- salem* (i. e. after its destruction by the Ba- bylonians) *unto Messiah the prince, shall be seven weeks, and threescore and two weeks* * *: the street shall be built again,*

---

* In prophetical language, a day is reckoned for a year, or seven years to every prophetical week. This key is given us by Moses, Lev. xxv. 8, and Numbers xiv. 34 and also by Ezekiel iv. 5, 6 ; and by this it appears, that from the commission granted to Ezra to rebuild Jerusa- lem, until the complete restoration of the city, there were exactly 49 years or seven weeks. From this period until the first proclamation of the Messiah by John the Baptist, there were exactly 434 years, or sixty-two weeks. John's ministry terminated at the end of 3 years and a half, when our Lord began to preach " *the kingdom of God,*" and thus virtually, " *in the midst of the week, caused the sacri- fice and oblation to cease*" (see Daniel ix. 27) ; for he him- self declared that " *the law and the prophets* (i. e. the ce- remonial law—or law of sacrifices, &c. and the prophets

and the wall, even in troublous times. And after threescore and two weeks shall Messiah be cut off, but not for himself; and the people of the prince that shall come, shall destroy the city and the sanctuary, and the end thereof shall be with a flood, and unto the end of the war desolations are determined*." Such is the prediction of one of your own prophets; which not only proves that the appearance and death of the Messiah were to precede the destruction of Jerusalem and the temple, but also marks the precise time when, in

under it) *were until John; since that time the kingdom of God is preached."* And exactly at the end of this prophetical week, i. e. at the expiration of the remaining 3 years and a half, he confirmed the abolition of the Levitical law by the *" one offering of himself"* upon the cross. This ever-memorable event happened precisely in the very month which completed the 490 years, or whole period of seventy weeks, mentioned by Daniel in the 24th verse of the above cited chapter; and it deserves the particular attention of the reader, that Ferguson, the celebrated astronomer, who applied the principles of his favourite science to this very prediction of Daniel, declares, as the result of his calculations, that the " prophetic year of Messiah's being cut off was the very same as the astronomical."

* Daniel ix. 23, 20.

the person of Jesus Christ, he actually did appear. The same prophet also thus describes the great purposes of his advent; viz. *to finish the transgression, and to make an end of sins, and to make reconciliation for iniquity, and to bring in everlasting righteousness.*" And are not these precisely the very purposes for which, according to the writers of the New Testament, Jesus Christ came into the world, and which, before his departure out of it, he fully accomplished? Daniel predicted, moreover, that the Messiah should "*cause the sacrifice and the oblation to cease:*" and accordingly, still to use his language, has not "*the daily sacrifice been taken away, and the abomination that maketh desolate been set up?*" and has not your nation (to use the words of another of your prophets) abode "*many days without a king, and without a prince, and without a sacrifice, and without an image, and without an ephod,. and without teraphim* ?*" It was likewise foretold by Daniel, that the

---

* Hosea iii. 4.

Messiah would *"seal up the vision and prophecy ;"* and accordingly this prediction, like all the rest in your scriptures relating to the Messiah, was accomplished in Jesus Christ; for is it not clear that his favourite disciple St. John was the last inspired prophet? Did not the prophetic vision close with his *" Revelations ?"* and hath any one since prevailed to unloose the mysterious and inviolable seal? It may further be proper to remind you, that precisely at the period of Christ's advent, a lively expectation of the appearance of your Messiah in Judea, was not only current throughout your own nation, but even obtained in many parts of the Roman empire. Hence the rise of those *" false Christs"* and *" false prophets,"* which we have described, and the credulity of your ancestors in believing their declarations. They promised temporal deliverance, dominion, and glory; therefore they were regarded. They true Messiah offered a release from the captivity of sin and Satan, a spiritual salvation, and everlasting glory

Finally, The catastrophe which we have described is pregnant with the most important instruction to the whole world. From amidst the ruins of Jerusalem, a voice may be heard calling loudly and incessantly in the ears of all nations, and saying, " *Beware that ye depart not from the living God!*" whilst the insulted descendants of Abraham, scattered over the face of the earth, re-echo, in despite of themselves, the solemn admonition, and, in effect, exclaim, " Behold! pictured in our fate the awful consequences of apostacy, and especially of our rejection of the Messiah, the Redeemer of the world!"

To the British nation, between which and the kingdom of Israel, during the period of its prosperity and glory, there are so many striking features of resemblance, these solemn warnings come with peculiar emphasis and import. May the Almighty mercifully incline us, as a people, to regard them with due seriousness and

M

attention, lest, after having been exalted
like the Jews, by our civil and religious
privileges, to the highest distinction among
the nations, we at length fall, like them,
into proportional ruin and disgrace. The
progress of iniquity in our country is already sufficiently great, notwithstanding a
variety of encouraging considerations*,

* The excellent character of our beloved monarch—
the wisdom and harmony of his councils—the moderate,
just, and humane temper of our government—the purity
and equity with which justice is administered in our
courts of law, and by our magistrates in general—the
spirit of loyalty and unanimity which pervades the country—the patriotic ardour which is displayed in its defence
—an evident revival of the spirit of religion in our national church, and also among those who dissent from it—
the decline of bigotry—the cordial union of pious individuals belonging to different religious communities, and
their friendly co-operation in the same benevolent under-
takings—the erection of societies "for the suppression
of vice," and the increase of schools for the religious instruction of indigent children—the establishment of many
other institutions for the more general diffusion of religious knowledge in our land, and for imparting the blessings of christianity to heathen nations : and, above all,
the formation of societies for the more extensive dispersion of the holy scriptures in the world, and for promoting their translation into languages through which revelation hath not permanently spoken to man—all these considerations, and a variety of others which might be enu-

to excite in the mind of the serious christian very alarming apprehensions concerning the final issue of the contest in which
we are at present engaged.   Alternately
he trembles and weeps while he contem-
plates the impiety and dissoluteness of our
national manners, and the dreadful insen-

---

merated, we admit are not the features of a country for-
saken by the Almighty, and given up to be a prey to its
enemies, but are rather encouraging indications of his
gracious and paternal favour towards us.   Still, when we
reverse the picture, and seriously reflect upon the spirit
of infidelity which pervades, and the abominable immo-
ralities which overspread our country, it is impossible not
to feel that we are justly exposed to the wrath and indig-
nation of heaven.   The profanation of the name of God,
sabbath-breaking, neglect of religious ordinances, contempt of genuine piety, swearing, perjuries, drunkenness,
adultery, prostitution, &c. and such an inordinate pursuit
of earthly things as absorbs all due regard to those of a
future state, are impieties and vices that dreadfully prevail in the different classes of the community ; and
which, while they exclude from the divine favour the individuals who are justly chargeable with such enormi-
ties, are secretly operating as so many principles of dissolution in the great social edifice of our country, tending
to diminish the security of our civil and religious privileges, and to expose us to the dangers of an external hostility, against which our powerful means of national defence, under the blessing of divine providence, might
otherwise prove an impregnable barrier.

sibility which every where prevails, both
as it respects our deserts, and the successive manifestations of the divine displeasure against us. Without any invidious
comparison between the moral state of
the present and that of former generations,
we would ask, what is the fact concerning
ourselves? Can any one say, that a pious,
devout, and humble demeanour is the cha
racteristic of our times, or that every spe-
cies of wickedness does not alarmingly
prevail throughout the land? So far from
the pure spirit of christianity animating,
directing, and governing our conduct, is
there a principle or maxim of common
morality that is not generally and habitu-
ally outraged among us? What is the
national feeling upon sacred things? How
beats the pulse of society here? Talk of
religion; make only a distant allusion to
it; what is the effect? A repulsive silence, a frown, a sneer, perhaps an insult.
What is the national sentiment? What
are the constant topics of discourse? to

what principles do we make our appeal? By what maxim do we regulate our actions? Are they the principles and maxims of a spurious philosophy, of an arbitrary system of morals, of public opinion of custom, or the fashion of the day? or are they the principles and maxims of the religion of Jesus? Let daily experience reply to these questions. What, also, is our colloquial phraseology? Are not words and phrases, prophane, immoral, and antichristian in their spirit and tendency, interwoven in its very texture? and are not such as convey ideas of the first importance to mankind almost totally excluded from it? The word holiness, for instance, which is descriptive of the " highest style of man" here, and the brightest jewel in his crown of glory hereafter, is almost banished from conversation; and the appropriate expressions by which the progress of christianity in the heart (and what is a christianity that does not obtain dominion here?) are contemn

M 2

ed and ridiculed as fanatical! Nay, even an allusion to a general or particular providence, if it be made with becoming seriousness, is frequently conceived to indicate an offensive degree of religion. If these remarks are unfortunately but too applicable to the community at large, it is at least consolatory to reflect, that in all classes of it there are many bright and excellent examples of genuine piety and virtue. Still it may be said, what are these among so many? yet few as they comparatively are, they constitute the *salt**
of our country; and

> This " *salt* preserves us; more corrupted else,
> And therefore more obnoxious at this hour
> Than Sodom in her day had pow'r to be,
> For whom God heard his Abra'm plead in vain†."

The truly pious of the land, indeed, after all that can be said of our fleets and armies, and that is not a little, are the grand bulwarks of our national security; and the regard of Heaven to them and to their

---

* Mat. v. 13.   † Cowper's Task, book iii.

prayers, is the surest ground of hope that
we shall be protected against the over-
whelming destruction with which we are
threatened by the great scourge of modern Europe.   It becomes us, however,
to " *stand in awe*," to cease from sin, " *to
repent and do works meet for repentance;*"
for, although our existence as a nation,
and our institutions, may be preserved,
we have still just reason to apprehend the
less signal marks of the divine displeasure.   It is not, indeed, for blind and er-
ring man to estimate the proportions of
national delinquency, or to fix the time,
the mode, or the severity of national chas-
tisements.   Generally, however, it may be
observed, that the number, value, and
duration of the moral advantages which
a nation enjoys, constitute the equitable
measure of its guilt.   Judging ourselves
upon this principle, how malignant does
our depravity appear!   how greatly ag-
gravated our transgressions, how deeply
stained our ingratitude!   Still we seem

insensible to our deserts. The sky gathers blackness; we hear ' the distant thunder that forebodes approaching storms;' but no salutary dread prevails, no radical, no general reformation is discernible. An atheistical dissipation of mind, a sensualizing gaiety of manners pervade, and awfully infatuate the country. Dark and threatening clouds, at intervals succeeding each other, have hung over us for a time, and then dispersed; and we flatter ourselves, therefore, that we shall continue to remain unpunished*. Nay, from a consideration of our national means of defence and security, we grow presumptuously confident; and, regardless of the divine judgments, which are so evidently " *abroad in the earth*," we in effect say, like the Jews, " *none evil can come upon us*." The finger of prophecy points to the destruction of a second Tyre, distinguished above the nations for her commercial grandeur and prosperity; and Britain, unawed, ap-

---

* Eccles. viii. 11.

propriates the description to herself, saying not merely "*in her heart*," but by positive declarations, *I sit as a queen, and shall see no sorrow!* But how rash and presumptuous is such language! For shall not He who sustains and controuls the universe, "whose power no creature is able to resist," and "who is the only giver of all victory;" shall not he make vain the strength even of the proudest and mightiest kingdoms? "He that chastiseth the heathen, shall not he punish" nations who apostatize from him, under countless obligations to love, duty, and allegiance, with which the heathen are totally unacquainted? From this vain-glorious spirit, so fatal to the stability of empires, may the Almighty mercifully deliver us! The evils of this spirit are incalculable. It dissipates that salutary fear of providential retribution, which keeps nations in awe. It generates that headlong presumption which rushes into dangers, and that haughtiness which precedes a

fall. It throws wide open the flood-gates
of iniquity, and paves the way to a radical
and universal corruption of public morals.
If, in the revolution of years, under the
influence of such a principle of pride and
vain confidence, this last state of degene-
racy become ours, it requires no spirit of
divination to perceive, that the awful
doom of all great and ancient empires,
whose dissolution and ruin the voice of
history deplores, must await us also.
Then, indeed, the measure of our iniqui-
ties being once filled up, " *He that sitteth
upon the circle of the earth,*" and before
whom " *the inhabitants thereof are as
grasshoppers,*" may render our national
bulwarks, vainly deemed impregnable, as
ineffectual for defence as " *the small dust
of the balance,*"—and, as a final display
of his vengeance against inveterate and in-
corrigible apostacy, may send forth His
commission to some great and powerful
nation, which, copying the example, and
emulating the fame of the ancient Ro-

CONCLUSION. 143

mans, may convert our territory into a
waste like Judea, and our capital into
ruins like Jerusalem.

For "that effeminacy, folly, lust,
Enervates and enfeebles, and needs must,
And that a nation shamefully debas'd,
Will be despis'd and trampled on at last,
Unless sweet Penitence her pow'rs renew,
Is truth, if history itself be true.
There is a time, and justice marks the date,
For long forbearing clemency to wait ;
That hour elaps'd, th'incurable revolt
Is punish'd, and down comes the thunderbolt."

* * * * * * * * * *

' *The word once giv'n,*' "and mutiny soon roars
In all her gates, and shakes her distant shores ;
The standards of all nations are unfurl'd,
She has one foe, and that one foe, the world.
And if He doom that people with a frown,
And mark them with the seal of wrath, press'd down,
Obduracy takes place ; callous and tough
The reprobated race grows judgment-proof ;
Earth shakes beneath them, and heaven roars
But nothing scares them from the course
To the lascivious pipe and wanton
That charm down fear
With mad rapid
Down to
They
C

But all they trust in withers, as it must,
When He commands, in whom they place no trust.
Vengeance at last pours down upon their coast,
A long despis'd but now victorious host ;
Tyranny sends the chain that must abridge
The noble sweep of all their privilege,
Gives liberty the last, the mortal shock,
Slips the slave's collar on, and snaps the lock."

COWPER.

FINIS.

inen
of the ba.
of his vengeance
corrigible apostacy, may
commission to some great and
nation, which, copying the example
emulating the fame of the ancient Ro-

ImTheStory.com

Personalized Classic Books in many genre's

Unique gift for kids, partners, friends, colleagues

Customize:

- Character Names
- Upload your own front/back cover images (optional)
- Inscribe a personal message/dedication on the
  inside page (optional)

Customize many titles Including
- Alice in Wonderland
- Romeo and Juliet
- The Wizard of Oz
- A Christmas Carol
- Dracula
- Dr. Jekyll & Mr. Hyde
- And more...

CPSIA information can be obtained
at www.ICGtesting.com
Printed in the USA
BVHW092037281119
565088BV00009B/388/P